Secrets
of a Closet
Millionaire

Michele Ashby

Secrets of a Closet Millionaire
A Step-by-Step Guide to Financial Freedom

Copyright © 2014 by Michele Ashby. All Rights Reserved.

Published by Ashby Investments, LLC
Denver, CO

Library of Congress Control Number: 2014932931

Ashby, Michele
Secrets of a Closet Millionaire
A Step-by-Step Guide to Financial Freedom
Michele Ashby

ISBN 978-14904942-4-1

1. Personal Finance 2. Wealth Management

Book Design and Cover Design © 2014

Secrets of a Closet Millionaire:
A Step-by-Step Guide to Financial Freedom

- Shares the story of an unlikely millionaire
- Gives practical ideas to develop your own wealth and sustainable abundance
- Shows how to live without any debt for the rest of your life
- Offers proven ways to get well financially
- Presents methods to immediately turn your money outflow into inflow
- Sets forth five simple steps to financial fitness and freedom
- Exhibits how to turn debits into credits
- Teaches how to create and start your own "Get Well" program
- Provides everything you need to succeed in managing your own money
- Reveals how to keep more of the money you make for yourself
- Describes why it's never too late to start your retirement account for yourself at any age
- Explains the top five misunderstandings about money
- Delivers proof that money has magnetic energy and can be drawn to you

Written by Michele Ashby, Holistic Financial Guide and eProductivity Wizard, an accomplished financier and business advisor, *Secrets of a Closet Millionaire* directs and guides you to financial freedom within your life and gives you a compass for how to find YOUR way to becoming a millionaire. This book shows you how to break the habit of overspending and avoid the pitfall of never catching up to your debt. *Secrets of a Closet Millionaire* can change the way you feel about money and help you attract and bring more of it to you. This book can and will change your life *forever*!

Other books by Michele Ashby:
Modern Energy Matchmaker, 2011
A to Z Handbook for Investing in Gold Mining Stocks, 1987

Secrets
of a Closet
Millionaire

A Step-by-Step Guide to
Financial Freedom

Michele Ashby

Dedication

To Keith, my hero, husband and life partner,
and to Don, the master of the Get Well Plan.

Acknowledgments

THANK YOU TO POLLY LETOFSKY FOR MAKING this book come to fruition. Thank you for sharing your stories with me and for helping me through the process of writing this book. Thank you for your sense of humor, patience, encouragement, references, support, and friendship.

Thank you to my editor, Donna Mazzitelli, for the input and guidance to organize all the parts of this book and for believing in me. You helped me to see more clearly how to help others through telling my story.

Thank you to my early mentor, Russ Herman. You've known me since my early days as a struggling stockbroker and entrepreneur and helped me gain the courage I needed to reach beyond my capabilities and go for what I wanted. You asked me tough questions and never let me get away with not answering them. You yourself are a serial entrepreneur and creator of your own life dreams. Russ, your stories of winning and losing and then trying again, gave me faith to keep going.

Thank you to Susan Guthrie, my therapist and friend. You helped me through the grief of losing my daughter and got me back on my feet. You saved my life by being straight with me and tough when I needed it. You taught me how to love again, both myself and others. You introduced me to MSIA and all the teachings of love and light that exist for us all.

Thank you to Gary McAdam. You hired me as a rookie stockbroker and taught me so much about markets, trends, and how to sell investments to clients. I appreciate our long-term friendship and occasional talks about business trends and how people make and/or lose money.

Thanks to Frank Giustra, my friend, for your belief in me and ongoing support. I treasure your wisdom and mentorship. I consider myself as lucky to be in one of your circles of friends. You gave me a head start in my business, and I am so grateful for all that you have done for me.

Thanks to Don Mitchell for your endless love and support as a mentor to me and to so many others. You shared your rolodex, but more importantly your passion for people and how to show up in the world. You are a dear friend and mentor to me always.

Thanks to my son Johny for your ongoing love and support. I enjoy our time together and I am so proud of the man you have become.

Most of all, thank you to my husband, Keith who has stood beside me through thick and thin. You have encouraged me to take the risks and be the entrepreneur I wanted to be, while making sure our home front was taken care of. You are truly my hero and the best husband in the world. I am so blessed to have you in my life and in my corner.

Contents

Introduction

Why This Book Was Written

JUST RECENTLY, A GOOD FRIEND SHARED with me that her marriage of five years was falling apart. Her husband had a failing business, and while her career was taking off he was not able to share in her success and support her. I wanted to support her in any way I could, which I thought would be through sharing some of my personal experiences and struggles I had. I sent her this email (I changed the names to protect their identities):

"December 8, 2013

Hello dear Sherrie,

First let me say that I love you and I love Danny too. I am sorry that your marriage is not working out with each other. I know you have both tried and I also know that ego and finances can play a big role in relationships. Keith and I went through a number of rough spots ourselves along the way. Once we started being honest with ourselves and each other, we were able to work through things. It is really hard and took us getting some outside help with a good counselor to get us through the rough spots. I don't know if you guys have talked with a marriage therapist, but it might be worth your while even if you are splitting. That is your call because you know in your heart if there is room for a meeting like that with Danny.

I know (being part German myself) that we are very stubborn and for a male it is even stronger. I am sure he is devastated with the business as that is a very hard thing to go through. The economies around the world have been very tough even though they seem to be recovering. I found that once I let go of my business, the new opportunity showed up almost immediately. It was that letting go that was hard. It took me over a year to get the courage to close my company. After seven years of success, it was not working anymore and I knew it. I wanted to keep some of those earnings, so I decided to close the business before I spent it all on overhead that I would never recover.

Anyway, trusting and having faith that things would somehow work out was really hard for me to do. I am a control freak and to let go of the wheel was a challenge. Once I let go, then new things came in, in a very constant and manageable way.

Things were moving in a new direction. I was able to sell my office assets and get out of my lease over the summer. I got to spend more time with my son as he helped me empty the office and get things into storage. I was able to help him out a lot with his condo and get it remodeled too. I spent more time at home and with Keith. It went well and I was offered a job a week after I closed my business, back in June.

I am telling you all of this because I know that letting go can be very scary. It can also be very good for you and give you the space and opportunity for new things to come into your life. You have to make that call for yourself. Only you know what is going on inside of you. You also have a great family and I am sure they are there for you.

Well, good luck with everything and know that I love you and am sending you light. Let me know if and when you are headed to NYC and if I can make it, I will come to see you."

Sherrie responded with an email acknowledging the efforts to get her husband to go to therapy and his resistance to change and to letting go of his business.

I am sharing this with you because it is a real example of one of the many challenges we face in our lives through relationships and finances, or business, schooling, families, mortgages, bills, and jobs.

I wrote this book to help you with your finances, but I realize that this information can be more than just about money. I want to offer you the examples of courage that I and others have taken to get through the struggles of life and a glimpse of what can be waiting on the other side of those struggles. I want to give you positive support and hope. I want to be a good example of what not to do as much as what are good ideas to put into practice. If I can help you to make better choices, then this book has been worth writing. I hope my story will help you to face your own personal struggles in life, as well as with your money.

When I was young, I admit, I wanted to be a millionaire someday, even if I didn't use that term "millionaire" back then. I just knew there was a difference between the lifestyle I grew up living and what I saw in the movies or on TV. I could see that there were bigger houses than I lived in, opportunities to travel to faraway places, nice clothes and other things to acquire. All of us were exposed to this imagery in movies and television growing up, and I think it became normal to see these luxuries and want them. I was raised to believe in the American Dream, which was within the reach of every boy and girl. Getting to that dream was another thing all together. That is what eventually led me to want to learn more about money and discover what it takes to have the possessions and lifestyle I wanted.

As a child, I watched my father work hard and bring home a paycheck that paid our bills and took care of us. My parents instilled in me a strong work ethic, as well as risk aversion, because they grew up in the Great Depression. They did not trust that hard work would bring them riches; rather, it would provide for them to live a moderate life and always have food on the table and a roof over our heads. I was expected to pay my own way at an early age and to take care of myself. I saw opportunities and observed how others made their living. I did not have a career in mind when I was growing up, but I knew I wanted to be more of a risk taker than my parents had been, to try my hand at making a good living and to live the American Dream. I believed there would be enough abundance to become a millionaire someday.

$ $ $

This book is a culmination of what I and others have learned when it comes to managing money, careers, family, and life. I am sharing my story and experience with you to give you the roadmap to success with money and the confidence to change or adjust your habits so you can attain your own financial freedom. This book is meant to help you find your financial freedom, your personal definition of sustainable abundance, and to show you how to get there on your own using the techniques I will present. You can find your own path to personal wealth just like I and thousands of others have. I believe the chances of becoming a millionaire today are even higher now than they've ever been. That is why I wrote this book, to give people hope and support in becoming their own millionaire. If I could do it, you can too!

I have spent most of my earning years working with money—mine and other people's—and have seen a lot of different ways to spend those hard-earned dollars. Having a lifelong "mixed relationship" with money, I personally have tried a variety of ways to build personal wealth. As a woman in business for over twenty-five years, I have been fortunate to have achieved a number of successes, along with quite a few mistakes too. I've learned from both.

Through my years of working with many people and their finances, I learned that money is most often a very confusing subject. Almost everyone I have talked to thinks money will solve all of their problems, so they want more of it. Although I would say that money is not the solution to all of our problems, it does make life easier and less stressful when you are not preoccupied and worried about it, but the primary issue is really our behavior with money. Once we learn how to behave with our money, it behaves back. Many folks do not understand how to take care of their own finances and just live paycheck to paycheck. Most people have credit cards and use them for whatever they want to buy, or to stretch the month and pay for necessities. Many people have debt and are simply not in control of their finances; rather, the debt is in control of them.

Does this sound familiar to you? Do you feel like a slave to your money or your bills? Well, I am sharing my plan to help you get unshackled and free from your money worries and hassles. You *can* get well financially.

As we get started on your plan to get well with your money, there are some initial questions you need to answer for yourself. Take some time with these questions. It's a good idea to start tracking your answers, so get a notebook or notepad to begin collecting your own personal get well ideas and thoughts. Think about your money future and how you want it to look. Here are a few things to begin to answer:

- Is your relationship to money healthy and well?
- Do you exercise your money; meaning, are you aware of what you are purchasing, and when you reach for your wallet to pay for something, is it in your budget?
- Do you have enough money? If not, how much money would be enough?
- What are you trying to accomplish?

If you have a plan already, get ready to add to it. You're going to learn how to develop your own "Get Well" program. You are about to learn more about the key principles of how to have a better relationship with your money, how to attract more money to you, and how to make your money behave better too. How do I know? Because I have lived it, taught it, failed and succeeded at it.

I encourage you to know more about how to utilize the most powerful tool you have when working with money — the money you earn. Once you are an earner, the big question is what to do with those earnings? There are many who want you to spend everything you make and even leverage it to borrow greater amounts of money against your earnings. But recent events have shown the world that using too much credit, and leveraging to buy things we really cannot afford, is a bad way to build wealth. It is a bubble waiting to burst.

We are going to go into the philosophy of managing your money — why there are certain principles that work for everyone in building personal wealth as long as they follow them, and how each day you may be lured away from these principles by great marketing plans targeted right at you, the consumer. You have developed your own relationship with money through your life experiences—how you get money and how you spend it is a practice you have developed over time. What you do with your money is up to you. You make choices with your money every day. Most of the time you probably never think much about it other than the fact that you would like more of it in your life.

In our society, we all have some kind of relationship with money. We may want more money for many reasons—maybe we want a new car, a house, security, or a different lifestyle, all of which can be acquired with money. Human beings are the only animals on the planet that are attached to and valued by a piece of green paper with someone's face on it.

Money represents value to us—how we view our own worth as a human being, how we view the worth of the work we do, and how we view the worth of what we are able to buy or acquire with what we earn. Our wealth (or lack thereof) is affected by our behavior as it relates to our money.

I expect that you are looking for things you can do to change your life with your money right now. You most likely picked up this book because you want to get going and create a better outcome. So let's get started! Today can be the first day of your own Get Well program. It's your turn now to act on your own behalf, to get well and find your financial security, sustainable abundance, and even become a millionaire yourself.

Here's to your Get Well Plan,
Michele Ashby

Preface

How to Get the Most Out of This Book

THIS BOOK IS STRUCTURED FOR YOU TO USE in a number of ways. You may choose to read through the content and then go back and make personal notes. Or it may be better for you to make notes as you go along. I suggest you make notes along the way. You can do that right inside this book by using the forms and space provided, or you may use a notebook of your own to keep track of your notes.

One thing I STRONGLY suggest is that you make sure to fill out the budget forms for yourself. These will help you see where you are currently. Even if you are not a numbers person, you will want to get an outline for yourself of your current budget. Use a pencil so it is easy to change your numbers as you go along.

There are also online budget tools you can use, if that is more your style. They will calculate for you, so you don't even have to do the math.

The forms that you will need are provided in this book. I have put them at the end of the chapters that pertain to them and then again at the back of the book. This is your book to use as you please, so take advantage of the layout as it best suits you.

Now, let's get moving.

PART ONE

*Every Journey Begins
with a First Step*

Chapter One

The Meaning of Being a Millionaire and Having Sustainable Abundance

YEARS AGO, I READ A BOOK CALLED *THE Future of Money* by Bernard Lietaer. As a former currency trader, Mr. Lietear's expertise is in international finance and money systems. The book fascinated me because it was about money and global economics—two subjects that every finance major knows something about.

The part that made the biggest impact on me was related to "sustainable abundance." According to Lietaer, "Sustainable abundance is defined as the characteristics of a society that satisfies its needs without diminishing the prospects of future generations, while simultaneously providing freedom of choice and creativity to as many people as possible." He adds, "The planet itself is sustainable. The open question is whether it will include us."

Lietaer goes into quite a bit of depth regarding sustainable abundance in his book, and it made me think about how it related to me. *How can I have sustainable abundance in my life? He is talking about the planet, the world, and societies all over the globe, so what would sustainable abundance mean to me personally?* I wanted to make this term fit me and become a part of my goals as an individual. Bernard Lietaer wrote that book in 2001, and I probably read it sometime in 2002. Over the past ten years, I have thought a lot about this concept and ultimately developed my own definition of sustainable abundance.

I was intrigued with the deeper, more personal meaning of sustainable abundance. To me, it meant security. It meant there was enough money that I would not have to worry about paying all of the bills or a mortgage or the tuition for my kids' college. It meant owning my own car, and it meant freedom and peace of mind. It meant taking care of myself and also helping others. As I thought about it more and really delved into what sustainable abundance was for me, it started to go beyond the financial realm. I realized that I wanted sustainable abundance in all aspects of my life—money was just one of those. I wanted ongoing good health and meaningful, sustainable relationships. I wanted to do work that I loved—and work that fed my soul as well as my pocketbook. I wanted to *do well* so I could *do good*. And I wanted to have a sense of my spiritual wellbeing. I wanted freedom to create what I wanted and the abundance to manifest the things I wanted in my life too.

For me, sustainable abundance means defining what is enough to satisfy my needs and the needs of my family. It's having enough to take care of myself so I can take care of others. It's having enough to live a balanced life while being grateful for what I already have. And it's having the freedom to create not only what I want and need but to do good for others while doing well for myself and my family.

Financially, what I heard inside of myself as I sat with this idea of sustainable abundance, and what I wanted, was to build a sustainable amount of savings in the bank to live on and to pass on to my family. There is an old adage that says "make your money work for you," or as another friend of mine put it, "make money while you sleep." These statements fit my assessment somewhat and made me think of how to accomplish my financial goals to get me there. This meant that I needed to be free of all debt and to have enough money in retirement accounts, or investments, to sustain me and my family financially. I envisioned that having this in place would afford me the freedom to live my life creatively and fully. And it meant that I would be independent of creditors and those who control the money.

I also considered what I would need in case the banks failed or the currency collapsed for some unforeseen reason. It was then important to me and to my husband that we own our home free and clear, so we would not have to worry about a mortgage payment. The next step was to have enough money in the bank for us to live on for the rest of our lives. Additionally, I wanted a safety net, just in case, and since I was a specialist in gold investments, I decided to invest a portion of our money in gold assets and diversify our assets into solid mutual funds so that the risk would be spread around.

Many people equate sustainability to the environment, and I am not leaving that out. Since 2005, I have worked with energy companies of all types, including alternative, green, and what I call modern energy. In fact, I wrote a book about the modern energy industry based on all that I had learned over a four-year period. Here in the U.S., we are gradually changing the way we use and create energy, and clearly, in a generation or so, we will be living very differently than we are today.

The new technologies in our world are bringing us closer each day into a much more energy-efficient one. We have the ability right now to become energy-independent as homeowners and even as a country. For example, as long as the sun is shining, solar energy is sustainable, and wind energy is available to us as long as the wind blows. New technologies are coming into place that will store up that sun or wind energy so that it will be available at all times. I have friends who are living off the grid and have small farm animals, like chickens and sheep, on their property. Communities have sprung up around the U.S. of neighbors who trade canned foods and other bounty that they have grown on their land. They are exercising what I call "sustainable abundance" and spreading it around. And it's working for them.

I continue to learn what sustainable abundance means to me as I go ever deeper into the meaning it has in my own life. I am currently, and by my own definition, at the point of sustainable abundance financially, so I am now developing those creative sustainable add-ons for myself. I have come to learn so much more about what that means to me, and I encourage you to learn what this might mean for you as well.

So let's pause here for just a moment and do a little exercise. Take out your pen and notebook and write down what sustainable abundance means to you. Get a sense of what it feels like to be supported in such a way that you have the freedom to be creative and are able to carry out your life dreams.

Now, imagine what your neighborhood would be like if everyone around you lived in sustainable abundance. Imagine your bank accounts and the investments you have in place to take care of you for the rest of your life and to be able to leave for your family. Imagine that you own everything in full and have no payments to make on anything. What does that feel like to you? What is that on your face—is it a smile? Write down what you imagine and how each makes you feel by completing the following:

My definition of Sustainable Abundance is...

For myself:

For my family:

For my work:

For my community:

For the planet:

Chapter Two

This Woman's Journey to Abundance

MY FRIEND AND MENTOR, RUSS, WANTS ME TO tell you about all the times I was afraid. When I think back, those times he is referring to seem so long ago that maybe I have conveniently tucked them away in my memory bank so I would not embarrass myself and also be able to avoid feeling sensitive about what other people might think of me. The truth is that I have had many fearful times in my life— even recently. Times when I was in relationships or jobs that were not working for me and that I needed to change. I have faced a lot of my fears and made some very tough choices, which turned out to be valuable ones. I made choices that meant hard work for me to follow through with. I hope my story will help you to find your valuable lessons so you can make those important choices in your own life.

I come from a middle-class family. Like most people, I started out working in an entry level position. And like many people, I worked my way up to business owner and entrepreneur. Along the way, I tried shortcuts to get rich quick, such as playing the options market. I quickly learned that the "get rich quick" ideas were usually a fast way to lose my money. So instead, I put my head down, worked hard, and paid my bills. I thought it was prudent and normal to put things and trips on credit cards in order to do and have more.

At various times, I either owned or rented my personal residence in an effort to maintain a stable environment for my family. I know I could have done better with my earnings if I had known the secrets of managing my own finances when I started out. I know now what mistakes I made along the way and can see how much of my earnings could have worked for me instead of being wasted on stuff I really didn't need at the time. The important thing is that ultimately I figured it out and learned to behave differently with my money.

I started out in retail sales and eventually became a stockbroker. With a high school education and a lot of guts, I sold people stocks that were being traded on the various markets. Later on, I went to a university and attained my degree in finance, doing that for my own personal satisfaction and to see if I had really learned enough to earn that piece of paper on my wall. During college, however, I realized that my real degree had come from the street—Wall Street to be exact.

As a stockbroker, I learned the markets and sold stocks to clients all over the country. I had become a specialist in gold mining stocks soon after I started to build my clientele. I liked gold as an investment and loved the clients, who were called "gold bugs."

That was back when there weren't many women working in brokerage houses, and even less visible in the gold investment arena. Some say I had advantages by being the only woman in a sea of suits. But I never looked at myself as having a greater advantage because of my gender. I looked at business as a competitive arena where I would be measured by my intelligence, experience, and reliability. If I saw opportunity, I went for it. Having a career as a broker was exciting, and I liked the challenges of the work I did.

When I first started out as a broker, the world of finance was new to me and really quite mysterious. I sold stocks to people who invested their money and expected their stocks to go up in price in order to make them more money. They lived by the old adage "buy low and sell high." Overall, I liked working side-by-side with the predominantly male population because for the most part they were predictable. They were there to make money just like me.

Early in my stockbroker life, I had some great male role models who helped me build my business and encouraged me to specialize in the field of gold investments. I wanted to specialize in gold mining companies, and these men supported me. I was given dormant accounts of clients who had mostly gold stocks and I was told to call them and see if I could convince them to buy more stock. I called those investors and learned a lot from them. They wanted more follow-up on mining companies and I did the follow-ups. I called the executives at the mining companies and asked the investors' questions for them. I was learning the ropes and becoming an expert.

That experience led me to other job opportunities later on in my career. I learned more about sales and business during my time as a stockbroker than in any other job I'd previously held. It was a great learning ground for me. Making one hundred cold calls a day built character, courage, and humility.

I also especially liked the certificates of appreciation that I earned—in the form of lots of dollar bills. But what I did with those earnings is where I ran into trouble. I was good at telling other people what to do with their money as investments, and yet, I could not seem to manage my own money successfully. In fact, I failed a number of times. At one point, I had to sell my home, move in with my parents, and take a number of extra jobs to pay my bills. I was a *broke* stockbroker—not a very good role model for my clients. I had lost my way from how I had been raised.

When I was younger, I had lived by a very different set of principles with regard to the money I made. I earned my first money babysitting when I was about eleven years old. By that age, I already knew that if I wanted something like a bike or a dress, I had to wait until my parents had the extra money to buy it for me. Once I started to earn my own money, however, I was able to buy those things for myself without the need to rely on my parents' timeline. But since my earning power did not go as far as my father's, I also knew that I wanted to move up and earn more.

I progressed up the youth job ladder of success by working in a greenhouse during summer and school breaks, and at the young age of twelve years old, I was already making a starting salary of fifty cents an hour. At the greenhouse job, I received a paycheck for the actual hours I worked. And I liked it. I enjoyed working and accomplishing something and then getting paid for it. It was a beginning—a fun job to have during breaks from school and during the summer months. From a very early age, I understood that money would not simply be handed to me—if I wanted it, I would have to work for it and learn to save.

My parents both grew up in the time of the Great Depression, so they always saved up their money to buy things rather than borrow money. They were very conservative and conscientious about their responsibilities. I remember one time in particular when our family went on a driving vacation from Colorado to California. My father proudly announced that he had taken $300 from their savings—the money they had put aside to pay for our trip. That was intended to cover five of us for three weeks. Amazingly, it did!

Those lessons were the way I grew up, and they shaped many of my decisions. For instance, as a young teenager, I decided that I wanted to go to a private high school, and my parents told me that I could go if I paid half the tuition. I figured I could accomplish that if I worked all summer and got a working grant at school to defer some of the tuition.

I went to that private school and cleaned the chalkboards every day after school. I also liked to ski, so I saved my money to have enough to go up to the mountains and ski on weekends. In my teens, I had mastered the management of my money to fulfill my dreams at the time.

After high school, I decided to buy a car and move into an apartment with my girlfriend. By then, I had taken a full-time job managing a retail store and life was good. I liked working in retail because I met a lot of people and I was good at my job. Another retailer tried to hire me away, but instead, I convinced them to hire me part-time so I could keep my full-time management job and work for them as well. I was up to about sixty hours a week at that point, but I was living on my own, driving my own car, and paying my bills. And I was living happily within my means.

My working career was interrupted by my first marriage and the birth of our two children, but I managed to work on and off throughout my marriage, continuing to add to my retail and management experience. At home, I did the household books, paid the bills, and ran the budget. My husband, being very frugal, watched every penny, and we had very little debt over the eight years of our marriage. We moved around a lot and worked hard to build equity in our homes—we bought them, fixed them up, and sold them for small profits during that time.

This was during a time of high inflation, and I can remember having a discussion with my husband about investing some of our savings into bonds. We chose bonds because at that time interest rates were very high, over ten percent, and the risk of losing one's principal investment in high-rated bonds was very low. I had questions about the bonds we invested in, so I called our broker and asked him about the ones we were in. I wanted to understand what interest rates (coupon) they were paying, the length of the bond, and more. Yet, when I hung up the phone, I was even more confused than when I had started. The stockbroker had given me complex answers to my simple questions and the terminology he used was way beyond me. I know this experience had an influence on my later decision to become a stockbroker myself—first, to make sure I knew what I was investing in, and second, in order that I would be able to explain things in laymen's terms to my clients so they knew what they were doing.

As my children grew up, I wanted to go back to work full-time, and that is when I decided to become a stockbroker. I saw it as a career instead of just a job. I knew that in retail I could only go so far, but as a stockbroker, the sky was the limit. I could potentially make a lot more money than I would if I continued to work retail. And becoming a stockbroker would offer me the opportunity to build my own future as a financial professional. I understood that I would be selling on a commission basis and it would be up to me to make it or break it. That was motivating for me, let me tell you. When you know you are the one responsible for the commission check you earn each month, you learn to plan, work, push, and hard-sell sometimes. Once I landed my first job as a stockbroker, I was on my way.

Unfortunately, my marriage was coming to an end and after only a few months at my new job, I became a single parent and a divorcee. There was a lot of change going on in my life at that point, and I was facing it all head-on. I was determined to succeed at my new career, to be able to support my family, and to be the best parent I could be to my two children. I wanted them to be taken care of and to know that everything was going to be okay.

Where does it come from? Why do some people have a lot more money than others? What do they do that is different?

Thus began my professional relationship with money—which led me to making it into a full-time career—through managing other people's money. I knew by then that I loved to work. And I knew I wanted to work with money and learn more about it—money fascinated me. I wondered: *Where does it come from? Why do some people have a lot more money than others? What do they do that is different?* I often asked myself these questions and many more. I studied financial how-to books, read the Wall Street Journal, talked to analysts and seasoned, successful brokers as well as business people. I was hooked. I knew I wanted to learn as much as possible so I could have more. I plunged in, and part of my initiation was to try some things with my own money. One "attempt" that stands out is the time I bought some stock options that almost lost me $1,000 in 35 minutes. *Whew!* That was a quick lesson to teach me not to do that again. I learned that I don't have that kind of risk tolerance.

Some months, my earnings were better than others because of the amount of stock I sold and the commissions I earned. This made planning for the payment of my bills somewhat challenging at times. I learned to keep some money aside each month when I did well so that I could manage to pay my bills when I had a bad month. It was during this time that I accumulated credit cards and used them to buy things when I did not have the ready cash in my account. I only used them for the "extra things." My paycheck was enough to, at the very least, make the mortgage payment and feed us throughout the month. Over time, I built up a good book of clients and was one of the top brokers in the country in gold mining stock, so I was able to become consistent with my monthly commission sales.

At the same time, I was scared to death to lose money for those clients, and I wanted to do the right thing and give them the best advice. That meant I had to be honest and not just tell them to buy or sell stocks so that I could get a commission off of them. As a result, most of my clients were "buy and hold" clients. They would sell when they made profits, but oftentimes, that took months or years, which meant that I had to consistently go out and find more new clients to keep my commissions and my earnings up.

Eventually though, after years of selling, I became tired of the commission-only business and was ready to move on. I craved more stability for myself and experienced tremendous stress when I had to rely on credit cards to get me through the month, only to start the next month deeper in debt than the last. I was a licensed stockbroker for over eight years, but after the first five years, I took my gold experience and started a new venture that involved the gold-mining industry. A few of my colleagues in the mining business had encouraged me to start and run a new trade association for the gold mining business, and we named it the Denver Gold Group (DGG).

For a few years in the beginning of DGG, I maintained my brokerage business, along with numerous other side jobs, just to pay my bills and keep everything going. Eventually though, DGG became a full-time job for me and was able to support me with a salary. I was able to drop my brokerage license and the commission-only sales job. I no longer had to start every month with $0 commissions or deal with the pressure of selling stocks to new investors. I had gained a wealth of knowledge about the stock market, and I had learned how investors tick. I had built a huge rolodex of mining company executives, and I knew the brokerage industry intimately. All of these factors put me in a great position to build something that ultimately turned into an institution in the gold mining industry and still exists today. But, let me take a step back, because I am beginning to get ahead of myself.

Back in those earlier days, I got into some financial trouble because I got behind on a credit card payment, and as a divorced mother with two small children, I was a perceived risk. Credit was hard to get and easy to lose. So, when I missed a single payment, I lost all access to my credit cards. The banks closed my accounts, even after I paid the amount owed via a Western Union payment. Although

I'd made good on my overdue payment, the result of my delinquency was NO MORE CREDIT. I had to figure out how to live within my means and make it on whatever I made each month. For the third time in my life, I learned to live within my means. And yet, I wanted credit cards and lines of credit. Why? Credit had become a crutch—I told myself it was for emergencies only, but the reality was I used it to buy things I wanted before I had the means to pay for them. I wanted to "look" like I was richer than I was. I thought it would make me look more successful.

Still, I was determined to get my credit back and started a guaranteed credit account. The bank LET me deposit $500 into a savings account and gave me a credit card to use against that savings. If I paid it off, and on time, each month for six months, they promised to give me back my credit. I thought I needed credit to survive, and it was embarrassing not to have a credit card. It was a status symbol and showed that I was doing well—or so I thought. I have since learned differently.

I decided to sell our home and move in with my parents just until I could pay off some bills. Luckily, my folks were receptive to my request for help, and I and my children were able to stay with them for a few months while I paid off some of my debt. I vowed that I would never do that again. After four months, the kids and I were able to move out. We found a small rental house to move into and started over getting back on my financial feet.

As I transitioned out of the brokerage business and started the trade association for the gold mining industry, I spent three years working both jobs simultaneously. I kept a phone on my desk at the brokerage office that was for the newly-formed DGG trade association. I had twenty-five-foot cords on both my phones and a fax machine in my office. This was ground zero, and I was building something new, something big. It was going to pay me a salary and give me the stability I was after. In the meantime, I still managed my 250 clients and advised them on their investments.

It took about three years to get the trade association going strong enough to support me with a full-time salary. Quite frankly, those years are a blur. With growing kids and growing needs, I took whatever work I could get outside of my two full-time jobs. I worked evenings as a personal trainer. I consulted for friends. I worked for florists during their busy season. And I did landscape work during my vacations. Whatever I could do to bring in extra income, I did it, and there weren't many extra jobs I wouldn't take on. I was earning money, and I was keeping the bills paid. I could have been saving here and there if I had known more about how to make things really work. But, I was doing the best I could to support the family and keep my kids in private school and to take care of them. They were my first priority.

$ $ $

You can tell by my story that I'd had a couple of opportunities by this point to live within my means—and without debt. My first husband had been frugal and very conservative with money, and we had no debt other than our mortgage. And then later on, when I lost my credit cards and was forced to live without them for a time, I chose to build my credit back up so I could have them all over again.

What was it that made me want to live with credit cards and continue to borrow? One thing was fear. I was afraid I might not be able to make it on my own. Having credit gave me a cushion—a false sense of security, really. I was led to believe through others that having credit was the best way to leverage myself and make more money, like making more money through one's home equity (this only works when home values go up). This was also during the time when ever-expanding amounts of credit were being offered to working people in our country. I received offers for credit cards in the mail constantly, inviting me to sign up and use that credit card for whatever I needed (or wanted). It was "cool" to have credit. It fed into the desire I had to have things instantly and not to wait until I could afford to pay for them. I was impatient and immature.

During that time, I had clients and colleagues who were very successful with their money. I worked with professionals—some were really good with money and others were not. I had examples all around me, and I was trying to emulate the successful ones as best I could. I worked with CEOs of the producing gold mines of the world and their biggest institutional investors. Over the next eighteen years, I built a solid rolodex of all executives and investors who became loyal members of the trade association I managed. I talked to them about how they made their money and what they invested in. I watched them grow their businesses, do deals, and make millions of dollars.

Pretty much from the time I began working as a stockbroker, I found myself asking the following questions: *How much money do I need? What do I want more money for? What do I deserve to be paid? How can I increase my earning power?* I remember sometimes still being short at the end of the month—I had more month than money. I would pay the minimums on credit cards and relied on bonuses and tax returns at year's end to catch up on the large amounts of debt I had accumulated during the year. This was not a successful strategy. I knew I wanted more money and stability and I wanted to get control of my finances. I just had not figured out a winning strategy for myself yet.

I tried different programs I read about, and some things helped. However, although I always learned something from whatever program or book I studied, I never really got to where I wanted to be. As a goal setter, every New Year's I sat down with paper and pen and wrote my goals for the following year. First and foremost, I wanted to be out of debt and make six figures. I knew there was a better way to manage my money, but I could never quite get there—to that place others seemed able to attain.

I look back now and see that I had too many things going on with my money. I was scattered, trying to do too many different things. I was not focused with my money like I was with my work. I was trying to fix too many things at one time—like my retirement account, the kids' college accounts, paying off the car loan, and possibly making an extra mortgage payment here and there. It was hard to tell if I was really making any progress.

There were many times when I was confused by money and angered by it. At other times, I was happy and grateful, as well as generous and greedy with it. I learned that money can be a very emotional thing. I think this is why so many marriages and relationships fail—because of money problems and how emotional we can become as a result of those problems. As I mentioned before, human beings are the only animals on earth that depend on green pieces of paper as a measure of who they are and what they have. Crazy, isn't it? And on that note, I admit, I have a huge attachment to security and money does represent security to me.

I was making a good salary as the CEO and Founder of the Denver Gold Group, but I wanted more. So, that was when I decided to start my own business and see if I could make it on my own. I started that business in 2005 and ran it until mid-2013. Being my own boss and a business owner has added a tremendous amount of experience, success, and fulfillment to my life. I have done well so I can do good for others, too. I was able to close my business in 2013 and take six months off on purpose, so I could take my time shifting into my next career of being a financial coach and productivity guide.

I have spent my career working with money—earning it, studying it, pondering it, creating it, spending it, donating it, losing it, and investing it. I can now look at myself as merely a steward of the money I attract. It is there for me to use to take care of myself and my family and also to help take care of others. This makes me feel great because I know I am doing well <u>and</u> doing good. I have learned that with the right plan and some discipline, my behavior with money is better and my money behaves a lot better too.

I remarried in 1998, and a lot has happened since then. We both had debt and car loans when we married, yet over the years we developed a program that has helped us achieve financial freedom. We had a hard start with money, and since we had both been married before, we came with a lot of trust issues about sharing our money. Initially, we kept all of our accounts separate and shared a household account that we both contributed to monthly for our expenses. Then one Sunday, as we were watching *60 Minutes*, we saw this guy, Dave Ramsey, who talked about how the credit card companies hate him because he tells people to close their accounts and cut up the cards. He got my attention, and I immediately went and bought his book, *The Total Money Makeover*. Keith and I started the program and managed to get out of debt in just over a year. Dave Ramsey's program became a staple in our household, and along with some other concepts I will share in this book, we still maintain those principles today.

In this book, I will share with you details of how we did it and how we continue to do it—how we found the answers for our situation. We started a budget, eliminated all of our debt, paid off our mortgage, and paid cash for three cars. We live on the cash we have saved. Each month, we manage our earnings with intense focus. Our money has a name and it goes where it is meant to go. Beyond achieving personal financial freedom, I learned about the Get Well program and this has enhanced my ability to get wealthier and to achieve even more in my life.

What I have learned over the years led me to a successful plan of action with money. I made some mistakes, of course, but I did many things right as well. I hope you can learn from my mistakes and not make them yourself, but if you do, take heart because there is a light at the end of the tunnel. You can turn things around and do better. I believe you will actually enjoy the process as you learn. I hope that my story and what I offer here will be an inspiration to you and give you the confidence to go for it for yourself.

Before we proceed, here are four questions to delve into right now. These questions are for you so you can take a look at where you've been and where you are at this very moment:

1. What is your work history and what have you learned about yourself from each job?
2. What do you tell yourself about money?
3. How can you change what you say to yourself about work and money?
4. What areas of fear can you break through to change your patterns with money?

PART TWO

Start Your Journey Here

Chapter Three

Living Within Your Means and Having the Means to Have More

AS I SAID EARLIER, MY PARENTS GREW UP during the Great Depression. I was curious about what their lives had been like during that time, and I asked them to share with me. They remembered experiencing as small children the shortages of sugar, rubber tires, gasoline, and money. They were raised to conserve on everything, especially their personal consumption, just in case things didn't work out. They lived on the land and relied on and treasured their communities for survival on many levels, including physically, emotionally, and spiritually. They grew up tough because they HAD to.

When they were older and started having their own family, things were better in the world, but they still conserved. They never owned a new car. Instead, with cash, they bought a used one that was in good shape. They never owed more than they had in the bank, except their mortgage, which they paid off in thirty years. Despite all of that, we never felt poor, because we had what we needed—a roof over our heads, food on the table, and some money for extras, like vacations, schools, or the occasional meal out.

My parents did not have debt and they had a strong work ethic. They were good role models for all of us and quite the norm back then. They started us out working part-time jobs when we were about twelve years old and encouraged us to save up for things we wanted to buy for ourselves. When I wanted to go to a private high school, I had to get a summer job and save up my money to pay for half of the tuition. And I was happy to do that, because it made me feel worthwhile. I felt valued for my work and for my ability to be a contributing member of our family. I was also happy that I could go to the school of my choosing. I appreciated the education that I earned because I had worked for it. It meant a lot to me that I worked each summer and every school break, saved my money, and paid half of my tuition for school so that I could go there. I was proud and felt I had accomplished something for myself even at that young age. I was already earning, saving, and spending within my means.

Years later, when I was a single mom raising my family on my own, credit was easing and it was easy to get caught up in the image folly of "keeping up with the Joneses." And so I got a mortgage and a new car, took a trip to Hawaii, and purchased lots of stuff I thought my kids and I wanted and deserved. I became a slave to the debt I had. The banks owned me, whether I wanted to admit it or not. And I still wanted more, more, more, and more.

I became exhausted and finally realized I needed to get out from under all of that responsibility and pressure of debt, so I sold my house, which was a relief because then I didn't have such a big expense in the form of a mortgage payment facing me every month. If I had managed my money properly and used more discipline, I might have been able to keep my house or move out on my own without having to impose on my parents for four months. That was not fun and came with a humbling realization that I was struggling. I worked extra jobs that year. In fact, I worked EIGHT different jobs. I swallowed my pride and went looking for any and all odd jobs I could find to augment my brokerage income and pay off my bills. I worked weekends and nights after my full-time job. Laser-focused and motivated to get back on my feet, I knew I had to earn that money.

I had gotten myself into trouble financially by putting charges on credit cards and spending money I didn't have. I was obligated to pay it back and got so far behind that I also owed interest and occasional late fees on some of my cards. I thought it was a status symbol to have numerous credit cards. I even thought it made me more valuable, but all it really did was get me further into debt and further behind.

These were tough lessons for me, but I promised myself I would not do them again. I had to change my behavior when it came to money. I was on the lookout for a better way to manage my earnings so I could live within my means. I was looking for the magic formula that fit me. I read books, watched videos, went to seminars on money, and learned something from each one.

How will I prepare for the times when I have an unexpected problem show up? How will I take care of these issues and not rely on credit? What is my plan?

What are some of the questions I asked myself? They included: *How will I prepare for the times when I have an unexpected problem show up? How will I take care of these issues and not rely on credit? What is my plan?*

I realized that I had to focus on more than just my earning power.

I needed a better plan, one that included all of my goals. That is when I came up with the five steps to financial freedom.

1. Earn (have a job);
2. Save (add to my "Just in Case" funds);
3. Pay Off (stay within a budget);
4. Give (tithe and donate); and
5. Invest (realize it would take some time to get where I wanted to be).

I started living differently with money. I was interested in saving money, paying myself first, and buying things when I was able to afford them, like my parents had taught us. I was on my way to a new way of living. I thought I was going to get there in short order, but it took some time. Eventually, I bought the bungalow that I had rented for those first two years. We ended up living there for eight years total, and it served us very well. I was still using credit cards during those years, so I was not completely out of the woods when it came to my own financial freedom. I had not yet figured out the web of indebtedness I was still caught in. And I was still in denial, telling myself "I pay them off every month, so I am not paying any interest really." I hear people say that very same thing to me today. I was unaware of how the energy and risk that the credit I hung onto could potentially get me back into fiscal trouble. I thought I was in control. That's when I met my future husband and we began to plan how to put our lives together.

I had this new plan, and I was true to it on many levels. I was making progress with my financial wellbeing. I had started a retirement fund for myself. I was making good progress. Yet, I was still not getting where I wanted to be. It turns out I would learn how to get there later on. The plan would become more defined once I was married and went through another financial awakening with my husband.

Together, we worked through our financial lives as a couple. We both agreed to follow the plan and we got out of our collective debt. We both agreed to the plan and we did it together. We had the discipline to follow through, do a budget, and live with that budget. It was hard at first, and we had our moments, but as we turned that corner and started to pay off our debts, one after another, we became happier and more in sync. We felt like we were accomplishing something together and taking back our power. We were proud of ourselves and we felt empowered.

We gained more and more momentum and we focused on paying off all of our debt instead of acquiring more stuff. We kept at it and paid off over $56,000 in debt in less than a year. And by the following fall, we had paid off the mortgage. We were debt free. We had even established a big "Just in Case Fund." We were not fighting about money anymore. We were on the same page and going in the same direction together, and it felt wonderful. It changed our lives.

By the time we got on the plan and were living the five steps to financial freedom, I had started my own business and subsequently met Don, who you will meet in Section Four of this book. It was during that first meeting with Don that I learned about the "Get Well Plan." The Get Well Plan was the next phase in managing our finances for life.

Before we go any further, let's take a look at some of the basics necessary to move toward financial freedom:

1. Are you ready to change your financial life?
2. Do you have the capability to begin to live by the five steps outlined above?
3. How might you change your own current plan and add these five steps into your life?
4. Would you like to know more about how these steps work? We will get to them in Part Three of this book.

Chapter Four

The Money Magnet and Mad Money

I HAVE LEARNED A LOT FROM OTHER MONEY experts. I read a lot and try things until I find what works for me. If something stops working, I look for something else. I suggest you read as much about business and finances as you can. Some of the books I have read and especially liked include *Think and Grow Rich* by Napoleon Hill, *The Snowball: Warren Buffett and the Business of Life* by Alice Schroeder, and *Richard Branson: The Inside Story* by Mick Brown. I have watched *The Secret* a few dozen times and interviewed hundreds of wealthy individuals about how they made their money and what they did with it once they made it. I am an avid follower of Dave Ramsey, and I have tuned into Suze Orman, Craemer, CNBC, MarketWatch, and other money shows and webcasts too.

I am a financial nerd—I admit it. What is tried and true for me is that credit and debt are not the way to true wealth. They have not worked for me personally or in my business. Yes, I have been blessed with a lot of successes, but I also have worked hard and long to get here. Along the way, I've had and used a plan and, when necessary and appropriate, I've modified it.

Recently, I had coffee with a new acquaintance, and she told me that she had worked hard for more than a decade and yet she was no further ahead than when she started. *How was it possible that she was still worried about money and living from paycheck to paycheck?* She was baffled by it herself. After talking further, it was clear to me that she did not have a plan. She had not been proactive with her money, so although she never seemed to have enough, in actuality, she was simply not sure where it went every month.

I have made mistakes and had failures, owed money and acquired loans I had to pay back, and I have learned from all of that. I am sharing this with you to encourage you to learn as much as you can for yourself so you can take control of your money. With whatever you read, including this book, take the ideas that work for you and use them to your advantage. I have accumulated years of tips and ideas about money and used them for my benefit. It is an individual thing. It is not one size fits all; rather, it is determining what your custom plan needs to be. I am not

I am sharing this with you to encourage you to learn as much as you can for yourself so you can take control of your money.

saying that you should deviate from the basics of *earn, save, pay off, give, and invest,* which I will cover in great depth in Part Three. I am saying that there are various ways to do those things and that in your individual development you should put together for yourself what will work best for you within those general steps.

There is nothing new being presented in this book; there is just practice. And practice makes perfect. Having a relationship with your money can be painful or profitable— it's up to you. You are the one driving the boat here. You are the one in charge of your money and your destiny. You may be facing some difficulties in your work, or health, or any assortment of life issues. Everyone has challenges. Yet, I believe it is important for us to get up and do the best we can every day with what we have. That really is all we are asked to do. Get up, get going, and do our best.

$ $ $

Things change; they always will. Yet, we still have choices. What choices do you make with your money? What works for you? What is peace of mind worth to you? To me, it is priceless to have peace of mind. Having a debt-free life helps alleviate a lot of stress. Living without a house payment is a fantastic feeling. It brings in freedom and more choices.

So, here are a couple of things I do that really help my success each month to stay on track. In a bit we will talk about tithing, which is 10% of your gross income and is the first thing to pay out. The very next thing I do is called my "Magnet Money." This is another tip I learned from a great spiritual leader named John Roger. He wrote an article about the Money Magnet, and when I read it I realized that this was truly meant for me. I like the idea of paying myself first and for years could not seem to get that done. But with a money magnet, I learned that the cash I took out was easier to keep for myself than putting money into a savings account that I would later withdraw from and spend on something at some point, which then destroyed the magnetism of my money.

So how does the money magnet work? I take 10% of my net income in cash every time I get paid. That cash goes into an envelope that I keep in a safe place at home or in the safe deposit box, where I allow it to accumulate. I save it up, and it grows each month. What do I use it for? Well, I keep it until something comes along that is a long-term investment I know will be an asset that will increase in value—something like gold coins, real estate investments, or rare art. I look for something tangible to put my money into. And something that I think will grow in value over time.

Recently, we remodeled our kitchen and our magnet money paid for all of the premium appliances we wanted—$25,000 worth. The new kitchen upgrade was a value added to our current home, representing an investment for the long term—something that will grow in value, something we can enjoy for many years to come since we plan to stay in our home. This was an added asset to our home and our lifestyle. And we did it all without borrowing a dime, leaving us with no obligation other than to enjoy and use it. Money magnet can do lots of things for you—it will suit your needs when the time comes and the assets present themselves. You can make it work for you.

The other thing I do regularly is what I call "Mad Money." Each month when my husband and I get paid, I go to the bank and get a set amount of cash for our groceries, gas for the car, mad money, and money magnet envelopes. We each get $250 mad money every month. I determined that amount because it fit into our budget. Remember that saying to pay yourself first? It comes in here. That cash is ours to spend on whatever we want, and we don't have to be accountable for it to each other. This is a little freedom cash that is much appreciated and fun to have in the wallet. I like having cash to spend on things I want at a moment's notice and so does my husband.

I also find that when I pay cash for everything I buy in stores (including groceries and gas) I have a better sense of what things really cost and how fast money can be spent. I want to be more frugal and conscious of what I do with my money when I use cash. It works! When my money has a name, it behaves differently.

I picked up both of these tips from others; and through the practice of using these methods I have found great peace of mind and tons of fun with my money.

Set up your money magnet and mad money in your monthly budget (which we will cover in the next chapter) and get started this month.

1. Are you ready to start your money magnet fund?
2. Are you willing to use cash each month and give yourself some mad money to have—guilt-free?
3. Do you believe in the energetic pull of cash in hand?

Chapter Five

How to Have More Money

DOES YOUR MONEY HAVE A NAME? DO YOU have a budget? When you make a budget, you give your money names, e.g., mortgage payment, food, gas, insurance, and so on. Until you make a budget and name your money, you will not be able to have more money in your bank account. Only a properly planned-out budget will give you more money in your bank account.

What do I mean by a properly planned-out budget? I am referring to one that accounts for all of your earnings each month and includes all of your expenses, including those that are beyond the normal, routine expenses. For instance, costs associated with holidays, birthdays, and weddings. There are other things too—health/car/home insurance, car repairs and replacement, tuitions, vacations, and home improvements all fall into this category.

The number one expense I find that people do not account for is food and eating out. Until they sit down to do a budget, most people do not know

The number one expense I find that people do not account for is food and eating out.

how much they spend each month just to feed themselves and their families. Our *hurried up* lifestyles have made it very attractive to buy food that is easy to prepare or already cooked for us. If we pay for that with a credit or debit card, we rarely know what the total is at the end of the month. So let's start with food. Figure out how much you spend on food and restaurants by saving and collecting all of your receipts for one month. Add those up and see where you stand. Plug this number into your budget and imagine paying for all of your food with cash next month.

It's essential that you put a label on each dollar before it comes in the door by putting a budget on paper. It's important to plan ahead for your money so it does not go wandering away from you on its own. You want it to be in your control and under your program, not anyone else's. Your earnings are just that—YOUR EARNINGS. Overall, I find it liberating to know where my money goes each month. That way, instead of my money flying out of my account and leaving me to wonder where it all went, I spend it on purpose. When you plan well, you will have more money in your bank account.

It takes time and focus to put together a proper budget, but today it is easier than ever because of computers and the Internet. I prefer the old-fashioned paper kind of budget, but online ones are easy to get and simple to update and maintain. For example, Microsoft Word has budget templates you can use for personal or business, or you can search for budget forms online and you will get a number of options there. Fill one out and print it so you have a hard copy.

If you decide to make your own budget or use the one included in this chapter, be sure to itemize every expense you can think of. Our sample budget will give you an idea about the main categories to include. If this process seems overwhelming for you, then prepare a simple budget first, expand on it later, and get into more details as you work the program. You should do your budget every month because you will have adjustments and it is important to make sure you course-correct each month to stay on track. You want to be as accurate as possible with your list of expenses so you can see where your money is going. You might find some surprises there.

A simple budget consists of a number you put at the top of each category, such as rent/mortgage expenses, food expenses, auto expenses, medical expenses, etc. Sometimes it is easier to do the simple budget first and then break out the expenses under each category later, after you become more comfortable with budgeting.

The security of your financial information is extremely important to consider. As you work with online and electronic resources, be sure to keep your budgets and financial information in secure files on your computer and do not store the full account numbers in the same file.

Security of your funds is important too, so it is a good idea to have fraud insurance in case anyone hacks into yours or someone else's accounts where your personal data is kept on file. Identity theft is on the rise, so a good insurance policy is imperative these days to protect your holdings.

THE BUDGET

The first step in creating your budget is to list your income from any and all sources. If you are married, be sure to list all income from both of you and total that at the top of your budget. Your goal is to complete a budget and fill in as many fields as you can. Your job is to get your budget to $0. Remember to pay yourself first. Include your mad money and money magnet amounts into your budget.

Here is another important tip—use cash to pay for as much as you can. Include in your budget the amount of cash you will need for the following month and make yourself a cheat sheet to follow throughout the month (see example at the end of this chapter), listing your anticipated needs. Once you have figured out how much cash you will need for the upcoming month and have your cheat sheet as a reference, you take out that amount of cash, which represents what you have budgeted to pay for food, gas, coffee, and miscellaneous compulsive items you may want to get during the month. By paying cash for everything you buy, you know you are done buying when you run out of cash.

By using this practice, I have had to learn to pace myself during the month to make sure that I have budgeted enough money for my household. This is a simple system that we learned from Dave Ramsey. I separate the cash into the basic categories to be covered. For instance, I put the money for our food and gas in separate envelopes and pull money out of those envelopes as we need it. Each month the cash is replenished on payday.

I currently have a couple who are clients in my financial coaching business and do everything online. They even set up checks that are generated each month from the bank to pay expenses via online banking. For outside purchases, they use a debit card. My clients were resistant to switching to cash for some of their purchases, especially for certain expenses such as groceries and restaurants, but agreed to give it a try for a few of their other expenses. They continue to use their online services and debit card but are now taking cash out to handle some of the monthly expenditures. To date, they have reported more awareness of their spending when they use cash. They say money is more real to them now. This simple shift has begun to show them exactly what happens to their hard-earned money and has increased the value of those earnings in their minds.

It hurts more when I pay cash for things than when I used to pay with a credit card (with the card it hurts much more later). I use a debit card for travel and online purchases, but otherwise, I am a cash-only person. This system has worked for our family and keeps us debt free and within our properly-planned budget.

I also have a goal to write as few checks as possible each month. I strive to pay bills annually whenever possible so that I only have to write one check instead of four quarterly or twelve monthly ones. I personally don't like online payments and opt for making payments by check because I don't want anyone else to have access to my bank account. If a vendor gets hacked and has all of my banking details, it would require me to change accounts and notify all of the online payees that I no longer have money in the account they are trying to get paid from. This could take months, and in the meantime, someone else might have access to my money. I am not interested in that.

"Simple" can truly make life easier and less complicated.

Before moving on, take a few moments to answer the following questions:

1. Will you take the time to make yourself a budget?
2. Do you believe that writing a budget will help you keep more of your money? If not, why not?
3. Are you willing to calendar time with your partner or a trusted friend, someone you know who will help to hold you accountable to a budget?

Budget Worksheet

As a starter, use this form for your simple budget. There are online budgets you can use by going to the Internet and searching for budget forms. Some of them track your expenses and income month by month and others do one monthly budget that you will need to update each month.

Remember to add in your annual expenses of insurance payments or taxes—anything you pay on a semi-annual or annual basis. Divide that amount by six or twelve months, whichever applies, and put an amount into your monthly budget. This is where you give your money a name.

You want to "spend" all of your income on this form, so write in any additional items to get you there—your "just in case" fund, mad money, and magnet money, as well as medical bills, gym dues, and other items that are not listed here but show up in your monthly expenses. If you are able to get this down on paper and review it with your family, partner, or financial helper, you are much more likely to stick to your plan and spend less, get out of debt, and save more. Good luck!

SIMPLE BUDGET

INCOME

Paycheck 1	$_____
Paycheck 2	$_____
Extra income 1	$_____
Extra income 2	$_____
TOTAL	$_____

EXPENSES

Rent/Mortgage payment	$_____
Household expenses	$_____
Food	$_____
Groceries and restaurants	$_____
Auto expenses	$_____
Loan	$_____
Gas and service	$_____

Credit card payments

Credit Card 1	$_____
Credit Card 2	$_____
Credit Card 3	$_____
Credit Card 4	$_____
Credit Card 5	$_____
Other lines of credit	$_____

Other expenses	$_____
TOTAL	$_____
Balance	$0

Example of a Cheat Sheet for Monthly Deposits of Income

I set this up at the beginning of each year and adjust it, if and when necessary. I make numerous copies and have them in a handy place to grab the first of each month on payday, so I know where all my money will go and ensure that it gets there.

Monthly Cheat Sheet

Example of a Cheat Sheet for monthly deposits of income:

John's Check

Gross Monthly Income	$4,500
Net Monthly Income	$3,192.80
Cash taken**	$1,519
Deposit checking	$1,173.80
Deposit savings	$500

** Cash breakdown for the month

Money Magnet (10%) of net	$319
Mad Money	$200
Food	$800
Gas	$200

Your Cheat Sheet:

Gross Monthly Income	$_____
Net Monthly Income	$_____
Cash taken**	$_____
Deposit checking	$_____
Deposit savings	$_____
Other_____	$_____

** Cash breakdown for the month

Money Magnet (10%) of net	$_____
Mad Money	$_____
Food	$_____
Gas	$_____
Other_____	$_____

PART THREE

The Five Steps –
A Precursor to the Get Well Plan

Chapter Six

Simple Steps to Your Sustainable Abundance

IN THE FOLLOWING CHAPTERS, I WILL OUT-line for you the five simple steps to financial freedom. These five steps are the culmination of trial and error on my part to discover a winning formula. As I've stated earlier, I am a financial nerd. Having worked with and around money and stock markets, I have learned a lot from books, people, and experience about how to handle money and deal with it.

I would love to be able to say that I discovered all of these tips on my own, but the reality is that I have read probably every book on personal money management, took multiple seminars, listened to CD's and interviewed hundreds of people to find the simple steps that have ultimately worked for me. Through this process of learning and trying different things, I made my share of mistakes. But I kept going and continued to try new things until I found what worked.

Those mistakes helped me find the solutions that paid off. I know these solutions and suggestions will be effective for you, too, if you apply them.

Achieving one's financial wellbeing and sustainable abundance in life is doable, and I want to help you find yours, whether it is monetary or otherwise. We live in a country where it is possible for anyone to attain financial freedom. There is tremendous abundance available here in the U.S. for every citizen. For those of us who are able to accomplish this, we can also reach back and help others attain their freedom from worry and stress regarding money and their future. In doing this, we can make a huge difference for ourselves as well as for our communities.

We live in a country where it is possible for anyone to attain financial freedom.

The following chapters are an introduction to the five steps to your financial freedom: **Earn, Save, Pay Off, Give**, and **Invest**. Let's take a look at the five simple steps, one at a time.

Chapter Seven

Earn

STEP ONE: EARN

The first thing you need is one or more jobs. Yes, I said more than one job. It won't kill you. It might prevent you from spending more money on stuff you don't need, but it won't kill you. It will help turn that energy of your money from outgo to inflow.

If you have a good paying job but no money in the bank, then you are still reading the right section. Give the money you earn a name. There is a name for your money when you give it an assignment. This is called the budget, which we discussed in Chapter Five, and it is how you direct your money each month before you get paid. That way your money knows what to do with itself and you don't have to worry or stress about it anymore.

Your earnings will dictate your lifestyle too if you want to be financially well. By building a budget and adhering to it, you will have direction toward your Get Well Plan (which you will learn more about in detail in Part Four).

If you are happy with your job, that is great. If you are not happy and want to change jobs, I recommend that you look for a new one while you are still employed. It is easier to find a new job when you already have one, because you are more desirable to a new employer when you are already working somewhere else. Be respectful of your current employer, though, and look for a different one on your own time. It's just good business to do it that way. I recommend a book called *48 Days to the Work You Love* by Dan Miller to help you.

If you want to get to your goals quicker, increase your income either by applying for a new job, asking for a raise, getting a promotion, or taking another part-time job at night or on weekends.

If you want to get to your goals quicker, increase your income either by applying for a new job, asking for a raise, getting a promotion, or taking another part-time job at night or on weekends. This is a great way to accelerate your plan. There are some other ways, too, which I will talk about later in the book.

1. Are you working at your full capacity of earning?
2. Are there any additional things you can do or sell to bring in more money now?
3. Do you love your job? If not, write down your ideal day at the job you would love to have.

Chapter Eight

Save

STEP TWO: SAVE

I encourage you to move back to old-school ways—"a penny saved is a penny earned" and "save money for a rainy day."

Recently, I heard a report on NPR that talked about the "Bank of Ben Franklin," referring to the amount of US $100 bills that are in circulation. Apparently, the US $100 bill is being hoarded around the world by foreigners. They look at the US dollar as an asset—liquid and holding its value to the point that saving hundred dollar bills in hiding places they can access at short notice is their choice for saving money and keeping an emergency or "just in case" fund.

I have always had some savings set aside—liquid, available, and easy to get to. I am talking about cash in the house in the form of coins and dollars. Even during my bleakest moments, I had at least $1,000 in cash on hand just in case I needed it. In fact, I called it my "Just in Case Cash Stash." This is different than savings in the bank, because banks and credit unions have hours of operation and you may have a cash emergency when the banks are not open. It is easier to get to money if you have it hidden somewhere in your house.

And if you are depending on the ATM machine for cash in an emergency, know that they have daily limits for withdrawals. They may also charge fees for withdrawals,

The money in your Just in Case Savings Account is money for serious issues, like your car breaking down, a medical emergency, or a water leak over the weekend.

and if you are in line with all the other bank customers who need to withdraw cash, who are also in some sort of economic "crisis," the machine may run out before you get your turn. This happened recently in Europe when there was a run on the banks in Cyprus.

I also have a "Just in Case Savings Account" for emergencies, which has a $1,000 minimum to start. Let me be clear—the money in your Just in Case Savings Account is money for serious issues, like your car breaking down, a medical emergency, or a water leak over the weekend. I am not talking about using it for school fees or a new purse you saw and want to buy. Learn to say no to things that can wait, and build the discipline to maintain a positive balance in your accounts. You will have the opportunity to buy those fun things when you get your budget under control and eliminate all of your debt (or use your mad money).

As we covered in the monthly income cheat sheet, you will be taking out cash each paycheck to cover certain things you buy, such as food and gas. Use cash instead of a debit or credit card to buy what you need. This must be part of your budget planning. You can use cash for food, gas, coffee, and other miscellaneous items each month. Figure out how much that is and put it in your budget.

Beyond the initial amount of $1,000 in the "Just in Case Savings Account," I added an amount equal to three to six months of income. As I mentioned, your Just in Case Savings Account money is in a regular savings account so you can access it quickly and easily. If my husband ever lost his job again (he was unemployed for three months at one point) or my business went down, this would be the account I would go to for our income. This calms me down and prevents me from having anxiety about money. Use your discipline to save money and it will pay off. Saving money feels good and helps build confidence inside and out. That confidence shows. When you have less money worries, you are freer.

When I have had shortages or sudden emergencies, I was able to pay those bills with money I had already set aside in this savings account. I also learned that I hated dipping into this savings to pay for unexpected expenses, so I would pay it back quickly to replenish the savings and prevent undo expenses as much as possible, only using those funds for emergencies and rainy days. Again, this is not money you would use for any known expenses you have coming up. Those are all spoken for in the budget you create, which gives a name to all of your money each month.

Get rid of your debt (more about this in the next step). Once those debts are paid off, you can put more money in savings and investments. Did you want a new car, computer, or anything else? Now is the time to save that money so you can buy it. Remember, living within your budget each month allows you to save up for those big ticket items you've been wanting and gives you the ability to pay cash for them. Cash is a good thing to have in your pocket or purse. When you see something you want or are paying for groceries, paying with cash is more painful and shows you how quickly those hard-earned dollars can go somewhere else to live. This can change your behavior. Working with cash, you might decide you want to stretch that cash and get more value, or maybe you'll decide you just don't need that new pair of jeans because you already have two pair at home.

To recap, I recommend you have some cash stashed in a safe place you can get to for "Just in Case" cash emergencies, and that you also have a "Just in Case Savings Account" with three to six months of your monthly income saved up for emergencies. Taking control of your money in this way makes it much more empowering for you when it is time to spend.

1. Have you seen the new hundred dollar bill? Are you willing to try some of the cash tips here in this book?
2. Are you able to fund your "Just in Case" fund this month? In sixty days? When?
3. Do you realize the importance of your "Just in Case" fund?

Chapter Nine

Pay Off

STEP THREE: PAY OFF

Pay off those credit cards, student loans, auto loans, personal loans, or even payday loans. "Never a borrower, nor a lender be."

I have tried all ways of managing credit throughout the years. I thought I knew about money and how to control my spending when using credit cards, but in the end, it just was not true. One method I used was to pay the minimums until I got a bonus or had a big commission check, at which time I paid off the entire balance. I look back at my monthly and annual records now and see how REACTIVE I was rather than PROACTIVE. My money was running all over the place every month because I did not take the initiative to tell it where to go.

Another method used by a number of people I know is to pay off the total amount on their credit cards each month. This method requires more discipline than most people have over a long period of time. A shortfall with this system is that even one medical emergency or shopping spree can put you into a position where you are unable to pay off the total for a month and then you are in the debt trap once again.

> **I look back at my monthly and annual records now and see how REACTIVE I was rather than PROACTIVE.**

Student loans are another major debt today. Kids and parents are finding themselves in serious debt because the student loans are readily available and easy to get. Students today can easily end up with a degree in something and a student loan debt of $30,000 to $130,000. These are huge debts to have to pay back and do not ever go away, even if you claim bankruptcy. I heard recently that student loan debt nationally is in the trillions of dollars. It has become the largest debt in our country, even larger than home mortgage loans. This is dangerous and not a good way to start out your professional life.

But how can you avoid it? Work more and save up the money to go to school before you jump in, or go to a cheaper school you can afford, or find a program that lets you use your work experience to get class credits. There are all kinds of options out there if you look for them. I managed to attain my finance degree at a cost of about $10,000 because I used my work experience to test out of a majority (95 of 128 credit hours) of classes. Those tests were a fraction of the cost of regular tuition hourly rates. That was a savings of about $40,000 altogether.

Getting to the point where I had no debt took years to figure out, but I finally did it. As I mentioned earlier, learning how to live within my means was something my parents had taught me. Since we had also lived that way in my first marriage, I knew I could do it again. I just needed a little guidance and faith that I could do it. When I read *The Total Money Makeover* by Dave Ramsey, everything I'd known previously rang true for me again. That old-fashioned way of saving before buying stuff that my parents taught me was right there in that book. I saw the light at the end of the tunnel and was able to visualize a sensible plan to get myself back on track and out of debt.

That is when my husband and I decided that the best thing to do was to get rid of all our debt. All of it! I wanted to *own* my stuff. I didn't want to lease it or borrow money to get something. I wanted to pay for it up front. I always thought it was an oxymoron to refer to my car or my house as "mine" when in reality some bank owned it. I just owned the paper—and on that paper, the bank owned it. I figured out how much something cost me by the time I paid it off with interest and ultimately decided that scenario was not okay with me. My husband was totally on board with this idea too. We decided that we were going to beat this together and then began to make our plan.

The first thing we needed to do was pay off our debts. It sounds simple, and in the end it was. We made a list of all of our debts and then started paying them off one at a time. We focused on each one as if it were our only bill. We started with the smallest bill first. We paid the minimums owed on all the others, and then any extra money we had that month, we used to pay towards that one bill. *One debt, one at a time, until they were all gone.* As we paid each one off, we closed that account. In time, we shredded our cards and closed *all* of those store accounts and charge cards. We learned to live within our means and to eliminate debt. We no longer had pressure bearing down on us because we owed all that money to some bank or credit card company. We owned our stuff rather than allow it to belong to a creditor. We didn't owe them anything anymore. We were no longer their slaves.

And if we could do it, you can too. Each of us has our own situations, but I am certain that we are all capable of living on what we make. We all have the capability of Getting Well if we want to do the work to get there. Are you ready to own your stuff?

If you are, then start here.

The following are the details for paying off all of your debt. Initially, create a debt list of everything you owe. Be sure to include all loans—auto, student, personal, and others— as well as lines of credit you have used and credit cards, even deferred payment accounts. List what you normally pay on each debt each month. Now comes the fun part—the elimination one-by-one of all that debt. Taking a look at the debt list you have put together and considering how much you are paying each month, you want to concentrate on the smallest bill first. Pay this off as quickly as you can. You will still pay your monthly bills and the minimum payments on the other debts you have. Once you have paid off the smallest debt, you will add that payment amount to the next smallest bill on your list. Be sure you go in the order of paying off the smallest debt to the largest. Ignore the interest rates on the various debts—only go by the amount owed. This is an important key to your success. Do not vary this part of the formula. The success you feel when paying off the smaller bills and moving on to the next one builds your confidence in knowing you can conquer them all eventually. Stick to the plan and pay off your smallest to largest debts in that order.

So, for instance, if you owe $800 to Macy's and the minimum monthly payment is $115, you will add that $115 payment to your next smallest debt once you have paid off the Macy's bill completely. The money you were paying to Macy's becomes "extra money," so you direct it to be paid on your second smallest debt—the one with the smallest balance now that Macy's has been paid. Be sure to not only add that amount to your monthly payment, but see if there is anything else extra you can squeeze out of your earnings to put towards that bill until you have it paid off.

Your focus is to pay this amount off completely and as quickly as you can. You want to be able to draw a line through that debt amount when it is paid off, knowing that you are done with it. Then, you need to close that account. That is right—pay it off and close it down. You do not want any temptations here to slide back into debt again. You are learning to live on what you earn, and you will be able to live without credit. You will.

If you are short on earnings or want to speed up your payoff, consider some ideas on how to acquire extra cash. Sell some stuff online or have a yard sale. Get a part-time job at night or on weekends. Bring in some extra cash and use it to get to your goals faster. Once you have paid off that next line item from your debt list, then move to the next one. Add the payments you were making on the previous two debts to the next one. Consolidate that payment and keep paying it down until it is paid off. Cross it off your list. Now move on to the next. And the next. And the next. Be sure to close down these accounts and stick to your plan. You will be living a new lifestyle and enjoying all that you have been working towards, because you will have the money to afford it.

This process really WORKS. It may take time, but it is worth the effort. Each one you pay off will give you a greater sense of control over your money. You are giving your money marching orders rather than the other way around.

$ $ $

Do you have a weekly routine of getting prepared for Mondays on Sunday afternoon or evening? I do. Sunday is the perfect time to take about thirty minutes and check in on your finances too. Pay bills, go over your budget, check bank balances to make sure you are on track, and make minor adjustments where necessary. Doing this weekly makes the end-of-month paperwork a lot less complicated and much more organized. Be sure to set aside this time to focus on your finances and you will be surprised at how fast it really is.

So let's back up just a bit. Let's take a look at how you get to be debt free if you are not there already. If you are debt free now, give yourself a big pat on the back for having had the discipline to get yourself there. You are in a rare and small minority of the American public, so be proud

If we all become better managers of our own money, not only do our lives improve, but the whole community gets lifted up as well.

of yourself and encourage others in your family, business, and neighborhoods to do the same. Even if you are already debt free, continue reading—there may be some concepts in the following pages that will make your life even better.

If we all become better managers of our own money, not only do our lives improve, but the whole community gets lifted up as well. Managing our money doesn't have to mean that we cannot have all the things we want. It just means we can have them when we can afford to buy them. So, pay off your bills. Stop money ills!

Pay your bills as they come in.

I used to wait to pay my bills when I got paid, and in the middle of the payment cycle, I would buy things and spend money that I didn't know I didn't have until the next pay period. Then I would be short. Now, I pay the bills as they come in and there is always money for them because I have planned it that way. My in-between spending is in check now because I know how much I have for compulsive buying, and my money is named—in my budget.

Have a positive attitude when you pay your bills, and be happy you have the capacity to pay them. If you want fewer bills on a monthly basis, eliminate the monthly payments by paying quarterly, semi-annually, or annually for things like insurance or property taxes.

Spend on your retirement too, but only after all your debt is paid off.

The next thing to consider beyond debt is your retirement. Do you have your retirement in order? This takes time to assess. You can be setting aside a percentage of what you earn while you are enjoying the fruits of your labors. You may want to look at investments, such as real estate or stocks and bonds. Now is your chance to invest in assets and grow your personal wealth and worth.

I was forty years old before I started any retirement accounts on my own. I probably picked the worst kind of investment vehicle a person could use for retirement, but I went for the interest return. What I bought into was an annuity offered by American Express. It had a guarantee interest rate of 8%. I paid in $100 a month for over a year before I realized that an annuity was a horrible idea. Since annuities do not have the beneficiary benefits you will get with an IRA-type account, you may not actually get back all of your investment if you die before the funds are all used up during your retirement. I stopped paying into it after that first year and my compounding interest built the account up to over $10,000, so I still have that small account as part of my retirement, but I am not contributing any more money to it now. I know it sounds confusing—annuities are a confusing product. I don't recommend them and would tell you to stick with simpler choices, like IRA accounts.

I realized that putting money into an annuity every month wasn't the worst thing I could have done, because it got me started and in the habit of putting money aside each month for my retirement. I had made a big step towards my own retirement funding simply by starting. I changed my behavior because I wanted a retirement fund for myself for later on in life. Since then, however, I have participated in 401K's, IRA's, Roth IRA's, SEP IRA's, and Simple IRA's. I have been aggressive in contributing the maximum allowed each year into my retirement accounts and into my husband's. I have invested in a variety of equity and market products that have allowed those funds to grow tax-deferred to over $1,000,000.

It is never too late to start saving for retirement. You just have to get started and put it in the budget.

I started late, at age forty, and I started small—just $100 a month. And I started with a product that was the wrong choice for me, an annuity. Despite all of these issues, though, I learned a lot along the way to give me more chances to build my retirement accounts and manage them better. Over time, as I stated above, I have accumulated close to one million dollars in retirement accounts at today's value.

How much do you need to retire?

Don't count on Social Security and the government to take care of you. Count only on yourself and figure out what you want to live on for annual income and then take that number and divide it by .08. There is a sample of the formula at the end of this chapter and also in the back of the book. The solution to this formula will give you the total amount for your retirement, which is your target amount for your nest egg. For instance, let's say you want $100,000 a year in income after retirement. Once you plug that amount into this formula, you will see that you need to save up $1.25 million in retirement funds and have a rate of return of 8% annually in order to get $100,000 a year in income. The closer you are to retirement, the more you will need to set aside each month to reach your goal, so the sooner you start, the better.

The first time I did this formula, I was discouraged by how big the number was that I needed to have for my nest egg. I decided to set aside as much as possible each year for my retirement funds, invest the money that was in the retirement accounts, and keep going. I will hit my goal a lot sooner than I expected because I have been consistently saving the maximum amount allowed each year and have invested it wisely. Combined, these tactics have helped to grow my retirement funds to almost my total goal well before I will retire. This is great news, and as I continue into the future, I will also keep adding those maximum contributions for my retirement. Life should be good in the future when it comes to my financial security.

As a rule of thumb, you should pay into your retirement accounts 15% of your annual salary, or the maximum allowed for each account (whichever amount is larger), each year up until you retire. You want to put as much as you are allowed annually deposited into tax-deferred retirement accounts. This will help on the other end when you are living on these funds because your tax rate will be lower after you stop working and retire. Although you may get Social Security after retirement, we are not counting that here. You want to have a principal amount in your retirement accounts that is large enough to sustain your lifestyle. The formula I have given you here assumes you will be getting an average of 8% interest generated annually.

Now it's time to spend on the big debts.

Pay off your mortgage. This gets you closer to freedom—freedom from loan payments—freeing your money. Aggressively go after that mortgage—take all of the funds you were paying for your debt and apply that amount to the additional PRINCIPAL on your mortgage. Be sure to mark on your payment voucher and check that the additional funds are to be paid to your principal on the loan. I have heard stories of funds not being properly allocated to paying down the principal on mortgages when people have added extra onto their payments and designated those funds for this purpose. Be sure to follow up and check to make sure your extra payment amounts are going to pay off the principal.

I chose to sell some of my stock to pay off our mortgage. The stock was up in price, and I thought the best use of it was to pay off the house. That was in September 2007, just before things started to unravel in the stock market and the economy. By the time the economy crashed, we were completely out of debt, owned our home, and had money in savings. We were grateful to be in such a good situation while knowing so many others were losing all of their assets. When the music stopped, we had a chair to sit in. We felt very fortunate.

The only right time to pay off any debt is the present. This pay-off process is fun and addictive—like a good game with friends, only you are the winner every time you pay off a debt.

Pay Off Your Debt Worksheet

HERE IS YOUR FORM TO TRACK YOUR payments for your debts, credit cards, student loans, car loans, personal debts, and any other amounts that you owe to someone else (everything but the mortgage). List your debts from smallest to largest, your minimum monthly payment, and the total amount you owe on each one.

Each month you will pay the minimum amount due on every bill, except for the one at the top. Your top bill (the smallest one) will be the big target that you will pay as much as you can towards each month—as much as you can afford. So, that means you pay the minimum due plus whatever amount you have left over from your budget after the essentials. And you pay this amount each month until it is paid off. Next, you take the amount you paid on the first bill and add that to your minimum payment for the next debt in line.

Each time you pay off a bill in full, you cross it off your list and add that payment to the next one until you have paid off everything. Oh yeah, and don't charge anything new while you are in this process. Get rid of your credit cards and use cash, checks, or debit card for your expenses each month. Follow your budget. Trust me, once you start this process and can cross off some of these line items, you will be hooked! It feels really good to pay off debt. When you are completely debt free, you will feel lighter and a lot more empowered with your money.

Debts	Min. Mo. Payment	Add-on Payment	Total Amt. Due
*List smallest to largest			
_____	$_____	$_____	$_____
_____	$_____	$_____	$_____
_____	$_____	$_____	$_____
_____	$_____	$_____	$_____
_____	$_____	$_____	$_____
_____	$_____	$_____	$_____
_____	$_____	$_____	$_____
_____	$_____	$_____	$_____
_____	$_____	$_____	$_____
_____	$_____	$_____	$_____
_____	$_____	$_____	$_____
_____	$_____	$_____	$_____
_____	$_____	$_____	$_____
_____	$_____	$_____	$_____
_____	$_____	$_____	$_____
_____	$_____	$_____	$_____
_____	$_____	$_____	$_____
_____	$_____	$_____	$_____
_____	$_____	$_____	$_____
_____	$_____	$_____	$_____
_____	$_____	$_____	$_____
_____	$_____	$_____	$_____

Debts   **Min. Mo. Payment**   **Add-on Payment**   **Total Amt. Due**

*List smallest to largest

Debts	Min. Mo. Payment	Add-on Payment	Total Amt. Due
_____	$_____	$_____	$_____
_____	$_____	$_____	$_____
_____	$_____	$_____	$_____
_____	$_____	$_____	$_____
_____	$_____	$_____	$_____
_____	$_____	$_____	$_____
_____	$_____	$_____	$_____
_____	$_____	$_____	$_____
_____	$_____	$_____	$_____
_____	$_____	$_____	$_____
_____	$_____	$_____	$_____
_____	$_____	$_____	$_____
_____	$_____	$_____	$_____
_____	$_____	$_____	$_____
_____	$_____	$_____	$_____
_____	$_____	$_____	$_____
_____	$_____	$_____	$_____
_____	$_____	$_____	$_____
_____	$_____	$_____	$_____
_____	$_____	$_____	$_____
_____	$_____	$_____	$_____
_____	$_____	$_____	$_____
_____	$_____	$_____	$_____
_____	$_____	$_____	$_____
_____	$_____	$_____	$_____
_____	$_____	$_____	$_____
_____	$_____	$_____	$_____
_____	$_____	$_____	$_____

Retirement Formula Sheet

TO DETERMINE HOW MUCH MONEY YOU will need in your retirement accounts by the time you retire, there is a simple formula. First, decide how much annual income you want to have each year when you retire. Let's say you want $50,000 or $100,000 income annually. We are not taking into consideration any Social Security income in this scenario. If Social Security is still around when you retire, then you will have a larger principal amount of money in your retirement accounts than you might need by then. At that point, you can decide if you want to take out less each year from your retirement accounts, or leave it in there to take care of your later needs, or leave it to your family or beneficiaries after your death.

Okay, so you want to have $100,000 per year income and you should calculate an average of 8% return per year on your investments in your retirement accounts. You might get more or less per year, but this is an average. Divide your desired annual income by .08 and you will get your number.

$$\$50,000 \div .08 = \$625,000$$
$$or$$
$$\$100,000 \div .08 = \$1,200,000$$

And so on—you simply divide your desired annual income by .08, reflecting an 8% return on your money. If you think you will get more than 8%, than divide your desired annual income by that percentage. In the example below we show what a 12% return would look like.

$$\$50,000 \div .12 = \$416,666$$
$$\text{or}$$
$$\$100,000 \div .12 = \$833,333$$

As you can see, the higher your percentage return on your investments, the less money you need in your accounts to work with. You should make this decision yourself, and I would suggest you talk to your financial advisor about the realistic returns to expect. I personally am basing my return on the lower end of 8%.

Chapter Ten

Give

STEP FOUR: GIVE

One of our most important benefits of the plan is to share your abundance. Tithing works. Helping others works. Giving to others is one of the most rewarding parts of making and earning a living. If you have traveled outside of the U.S., then you know that we are truly blessed with infinite abundance and have an incredible life here. Most of us take so much for granted and forget that there are millions of people in the world who don't even have enough food, clean water, or electricity. For my part, I have a number of select groups and projects that I support.

I learned about tithing as a child and watched my parents give to the church. I wondered as an adult how I would ever be able to give up 10% of my earnings to a church and how that might benefit me. Somewhere inside of me, I did want to give and I knew that helping others was something that was a part of me. It just seemed that 10% was a lot, and I needed to learn more about why this was the amount we should all give. I started out not believing that giving 10% was important and have come to believe that it is the proper amount to give and does benefit me in a variety of ways. I think this is a very personal decision for people, but I encourage you to learn more about tithing and what benefits it can bring into your life both financially and spiritually. As I mentioned, I consider myself a steward of the money that comes into my life. I am responsible to honor, value, and be responsible with that money to the best of my ability. Tithing is my first responsibility in giving back.

Initially, I was not always willing or able to give 10% of my earnings each month. I gave what I could, though, whether it was a few dollars or a check for $100 at Christmas. I made a contribution, and when I got out of debt and started living in greater abundance, I raised my giving to tithe the full 10% of my gross earnings. This became my ritual each month. I still tithe and believe in the practice. It is fulfilling to give to what I believe is the source of our abundance.

When I get paid, I start with tithing, which is 10% of my gross income. This is the first check I write each month on payday. I write out that check and put it in the envelope to mail it in and I put a smiley face on the check. This is my way of acknowledging the abundance that I have in my life and is a sign of gratitude for all of my blessings.

Through tithing, your church community or spiritual group will benefit from your ongoing support.

Through tithing, your church community or spiritual group will benefit from your ongoing support. If you don't have a religious affiliation, then I suggest you find some causes that really matter to you and begin to support them. When I can, I do both. I give according to my business earnings to other organizations and causes.

My biggest passion is to fund research for pediatric sarcomas (cancers), and over the years I've had the opportunity to help further great research in this field. Although it seems slow to me, progress is being made, and I am happy to have been able to fund some of that and will continue to do so.

1. Are you a giver?
2. What or whom do you give to?
3. Is it in your budget each month?

Chapter Eleven

Invest

STEP FIVE: INVEST

Here are some of the definitions of the word "invest":

1. Buy stocks and bonds;
2. Deposit money in a bank;
3. Spend money on a project;
4. Contribute effort to something;
5. Make a purchase.

Investing is a topic that is wide and deep, and what I want you to remember about this more than anything is that *investing is personal* and it is different for everyone. When we invest in something or someone, there are many variables in play on both sides of the deal. One of the primary regulations of investment professionals is that they need to follow what is called the prudent investor rule, which in the old days was referred to as the prudent man rule. This original rule was established in 1830 to protect investors from scam artists and fake investment products.

Today, the revised rule also serves as a guideline to help determine what types of investments are right for each type of investor. When you open a brokerage account today, you will most likely be asked to fill out a questionnaire and agree that your answers are truthful and correct. This is to determine your risk tolerance for investments and what you can afford to lose. For instance, I pulled the following questionnaire from the Vanguard website (https://personal.vanguard.com/us/FundsInvQuestionnaire). You might want to answer these questions for yourself to get a better sense of your risk tolerance for different investment scenarios.

When you open a brokerage account today, you will most likely be asked to fill out a questionnaire and agree that your answers are truthful and correct. This is to determine your risk tolerance for investments and what you can afford to lose.

Investor Questionnaire

1. I plan to begin taking money from my investments in . . .
   - □ 1 year or less
   - □ 1 – 2 years
   - □ 3 – 5 years
   - □ 6 – 10 years
   - □ 11 – 15 years
   - □ More than 15 years

2. As I withdraw money from these investments, I plan to spend it over a period of . . .

□ 2 years or less
□ 3 – 5 years
□ 6 – 10 years
□ 11 – 15 years
□ More than 15 years

3. When making a long-term investment, I plan to keep the money invested for . . .

□ 1 – 2 years
□ 3 – 4 years
□ 5 – 6 years
□ 7 – 8 years
□ More than 8 years

4. From September 2008 through November 2008, stocks lost over 31%. If I owned a stock investment that lost about 31% in 3 months, I would: (If you owned stocks during this period, select the answer that corresponds to your actual behavior.)

□ Sell all of the remaining investment.
□ Sell a portion of the remaining investment.
□ Hold onto the investment and sell nothing.
□ Buy more of the investment.

5. Generally, I prefer investments with little or no fluctuation in value, and I'm willing to accept the lower return associated with these investments.

□ Strongly disagree
□ Disagree
□ Somewhat agree
□ Agree
□ Strongly agree

6. During market declines, I tend to sell portions of my riskier assets and invest the money in safer assets.
    □ Strongly disagree
    □ Disagree
    □ Somewhat agree
    □ Agree
    □ Strongly agree

7. I would invest in a mutual fund based solely on a brief conversation with a friend, co-worker, or relative.
    □ Strongly disagree
    □ Disagree
    □ Somewhat agree
    □ Agree
    □ Strongly agree

8. From September 2008 through October 2008, bonds lost nearly 4%. If I owned a bond investment that lost almost 4% in 2 months, I would: (If you owned bonds during this period, select the answer that corresponds to your actual behavior.)
    □ Sell all of the remaining investment.
    □ Sell a portion of the remaining investment.
    □ Hold onto the investment and sell nothing.
    □ Buy more of the investment.

9. The chart below shows the greatest 1-year loss and the highest 1-year gain on 3 different hypothetical investments of $10,000.* Given the potential gain or loss in any 1 year, I would invest my money in:
    □ A (loss of $164, gain of $593)
    □ B (loss of $1,020, gain of $1,921)
    □ C (loss of $3,639, gain of $4,229)

*The maximum gain or loss on an investment is impossible to predict. The ranges shown in the chart are hypothetical and are designed solely to gauge an investor's risk tolerance.

10. My current and future income sources (for example, salary, Social Security, pension) are:
   □ Very unstable
   □ Unstable
   □ Somewhat stable
   □ Stable
   □ Very stable

11. When it comes to investing in stock or bond mutual funds (or individual stocks or bonds), I would describe myself as . . .
   □ Very inexperienced
   □ Somewhat inexperienced
   □ Somewhat experienced
   □ Experienced
   □ Very experienced

Your current asset allocation
Enter the current allocation in whole numbers for the savings used to answer question 10. Your percentages must total 100%. If you don't enter any data, the questionnaire will assume 100% of your assets are in short-term reserves.

Short-term reserves	_____%
Bonds	_____%
Stocks	_____%

$ $ $

There are many variations of questionnaires like this and examples you can find online if you Google "investor risk tolerance." This one gives you a good idea of what to expect when you are getting ready to invest in the stock or bond markets. As for real estate, the qualification process for mortgage loans and a good realtor will help you determine what is the best way for you to buy real estate and what is the best fit for you. Be careful, though, because if you are borrowing money to buy real estate, you will have loans to pay and responsibilities to manage and maintain your properties. In other words, you will be back in debt, unless you save up the funds to buy your real estate and pay cash. Other hard asset investments include gold, silver, art, and collectibles. All of these take expertise and a good understanding of what you are buying and the risks involved.

In order for you to invest and be comfortable, you really need to learn about investing or have a competent and trustworthy investment advisor. The topic of investing is huge and there are many resources in books, classes, and online resources. I have included a few book recommendations at the end of this book.

Remember that all of this takes time. I never was a patient person, and that got me into lots of trouble with my money. I was looking for the quick ways to make more money—shortcuts that would make me richer faster. Well, guess what? The "get rich quick" schemes are just that, schemes. And what looks easy to us or looks like an overnight success is usually something that has been in the making for many years. We are all an accumulation of our experiences. Even Facebook was invented because of an experience: his girlfriend breaking up with Mark Zuckerberg, or so the story goes.

Your time is precious, but we all have the same amount of time each day. Everyone gets just twenty-four hours in a day. What you do with your time is important. You need some time to work, some to rest, and some to relax or take care of others. It's a balancing act for sure. Look at your quality of life and think about how you allocate your time. Are you working too much and getting burned out? Are you sleeping too much and missing out? Could you be better at managing your time? We all have the same questions to consider—it's our answers that can differ. This is a choice, so how you spend your time is up to you.

When it comes to your money and time, you can get time on your side. Your money can work for you over time. Think of setting aside your retirement money for the long-term. Small amounts of money can become multi-millions over time, if you are consistent in your plan and invest in good solid assets in your retirement funds. The younger you are when you start, the longer your money will have to work for you, growing and multiplying. I suggest you look at good mutual funds for your investments and use Morningstar online to help you find good performing mutual funds. Look at how long they have been in business and at their return on investment year over year and on average. The funds are all rated, so you can see who is ranked in the top.

I look for funds that have a ten-year track record, with solid returns of 8% average or more. If this is too complex for you, talk to a financial professional. If you don't have one or know of someone, get a referral from someone who is a successful investor. I use Charles Schwab and pick my own investments. Then, I don't have bank fees on those retirement accounts either.

As you build your savings and continue to earn and save, you have more of an opportunity to use your time to grow your money. This is an important fact—the longer you are working, the more money you will have in retirement. If you decide to retire at sixty-five, you will have less money to spend than if you postpone retirement by even one year! Continuing to earn will guarantee you more money to live on during your retirement years. And your retirement funds continue to grow in your accounts with interest.

1. Do you want to do your own investing? If so, do you have the time to research and understand what you are buying and the risk tolerance for potential losses?
2. Do you know an investment professional you trust? If not, do you know where to find a good referral?
3. What is your plan this year for investing and what are your expectations?

PART FOUR

The Get Well Plan

Chapter Twelve

An Introduction to Getting Well

EVERYONE SHOULD HAVE A "GET WELL" plan. I have a great story about how I first found out about them and then built one for myself. It is a narrative about my encounter with a businessman who became one of my mentors. His name was Don and he lived in Orlando, Florida. We met at one of my resource conferences in Dubai. I was so enthralled by what he taught me in just one hour that I wanted to learn more. I wanted to know what to do with my finances to go beyond the basics of living within my means and being debt free. I wanted to know how rich people got richer and how they set themselves up for the future. I needed a bigger plan and Don seemed to know how to show me the way.

Here's what happened that fateful day. A mutual friend of ours set up a meeting for one hour and as Don and I settled in at a bar table with two chairs, he brought out a yellow legal pad. He wrote on it as he spoke, "Michele, I am going to help you with your Get Well Plan." I wanted to know what he was talking about. I had been living my five steps to financial freedom. I had done strategic planning, goal setting, program organizing, but I'd never heard of a Get Well Plan. He explained further by asking me what I wanted that would make it so that I was "well" financially, physically, emotionally, and spiritually. He told me to think about it—to take some quiet time by myself and put together my own list of what I wanted in order to be "well." This was bigger than just living within my means; it was about my future and what I wanted in the long run. You know that stuff we put off and really don't give much consideration?

What Don was asking me to do was to share my bucket list and my dreams. He encouraged me to write down anything that came up for me that was important. He told me to include fun things and expensive things, if they were on the list. He gave me permission to be materialistic. I was intrigued. I had lots of things spinning around in my head that day. Don explained that all I wanted was attainable and that he would help me with my plan. If I wanted, he would spend a day with me and give me his counsel for free. All I had to do was let him know that I wanted to follow up with this plan of his. I needed to get my list together, and when I got home, reconnect with him to organize a trip to Orlando for a day to learn more about the Get Well Plan.

Making the list was easy for me. It had been there just under the surface the whole time. I had simply been too scared to put it all out there—afraid of wanting too much, being too greedy, and failing to reach my lofty goals. But once I knew that I would have help from someone who had done this before, I was ready to take it on. I put my list together and then got back in touch with Don. He asked me to total up the monetary line items on my plan and give him a number. My number was $2.31M from that first list. Here is what it looked like:

Financial list:

Pay off home mortgage:	$ 190,000
Buy a Range Rover Sport	$ 50,000
Buy a Porsche convertible	$ 70,000
Fund my retirement fund	$ 1,200,000
Buy a mountain retreat	$ 500,000
Create a slush fund for homes	$ 100,000
Build garages for cars	$ 200,000

Emotional/Spiritual list:

Balance in my life between work and home

Respect and honor myself and others

Cure cancer – give more to research – much more

Respect my husband and our marriage

Reach my goal weight

Reach my full potential

My list took up one sheet of paper. I did not need to elaborate. What I wanted was right there. Your list is right there too. You have one inside of you. Don't be shy. Take out your notebook and a pen and begin to write it all down.

Set aside this book now and take some time to think about what would make you Get Well financially, physically, emotionally, and spiritually. Ignore any of those voices that might say you cannot do this. Just do it. Get it all out— NOW. Hang on to this piece of paper and put a date on it. You will want to see how great this works over time and track where you are in your Get Well Plan.

$$\$ \$ \$$$

I want to share with you the exact experience I had in meeting my mentor, Don, and how he helped guide me through this process. Don became more than a mentor to me; he became a dear friend and chief advisor to my company. I think, and you will see as you read on, that Don was also someone I had asked for to Get Well. I met him at a critical time in my business and personal life, at a time when I did not trust many people and when a number of people wanted to get involved with my business. I was not looking for any business partners. In fact, I was perfectly happy as a sole proprietor of my business, without the headaches of partners or a board to answer to. I had worked almost twenty years to get this far in my industry and this was my chance to really cash in and do my thing.

My husband was, and still is, my partner and biggest supporter, and he has been there through thick and thin, while Don buoyed up my business acumen and accomplishments in ways that my husband could not help me. Together, they have been my A Team, and I am so grateful they've been in my corner.

I encourage you to find your version of Don and ask for them to come into your life and help you with your Get Well Plan. You want someone who is successful, has integrity, and truly wants to help you succeed. They are not people who require financial acknowledgment or financial gain for what they do, but who do the work out of love. Yes, love. Love for business, people, service, and excellence. They are out there, trust me.

What Don said to me at the very beginning of our relationship, what really caught my attention, was to "get well." He talked about what could happen once I got well. He didn't necessarily mean physically getting well, but rather holistically doing so. The message rang true for me. In the back of my mind I had been saying to myself: *How do I reach my ultimate goals? What is the best way to designate my time, energy, and assets to get there?* I could see this road before me lined up with exhausting projects that made money for me but used me up along the way. I was looking for a plan, a method, a way to work smarter, get wealthy, stay saner, and find balance in my life. That's when I met Don and heard the term "get well" for the first time.

In that one-hour, one-on-one meeting with Don in Dubai, he drew some diagrams and talked to me about the "get well" concept. It's simple:

If I "get well," then I can do whatever I want. I can put all of my energies toward my ultimate goals and dreams. Those around me will "get well" too. I can work with those who have gotten well, are getting well, and who want to get well.

This is the best club I ever joined! **The Get Well Club**. I came away from our meeting in Dubai with a commitment to follow up with Don about our initial conversation. I had shared with Don my anxieties about my success and my concerns about how to grow my company from there. I also shared with him my ultimate goal (to cure cancer) and my reasons for wanting to be successful.

That is what I did, and I am here to tell you that today almost all of the financial items have been accomplished on my list. The date on my original Get Well Plan was November 18, 2006, so within six years, I managed to move $2,000,000 into my own Get Well Plan. I never would have been able

This is the best club I ever joined! The Get Well Club.

to do it without a plan and the support and encouragement of my friend Don. He taught me to believe in myself in a much bigger way than I had known before. He let me see what we are all capable of accomplishing and that there is a wealth of abundance out there for us to partake in. Oh, and along the way, I gave away over $300,000 to charities on top of what I earned for myself and my business. If I could do this, you can too.

$ $ $

I have a very personal reason for wanting to cure cancer because, along the way I had a family tragedy—the kind no one wants to have. In 1998, my daughter Daniele was diagnosed with a rare type of cancer called *Ewing's Sarcoma*. She was eighteen years old. She fought her cancer for sixteen months and went through numerous rounds of chemo, radiation, and a bone marrow transplant. Her cancer went into remission for four months. But, in April of 1999, she lost her battle and passed away. She always used to say to me, "Mom, we were picked for a reason," and after her death I tried to define what that meant for me—*what was my reason*? I was left behind to do something for a reason—to cure cancer. This event changed my life forever and became the reason why I left my cushy job with the association to venture out on my own to build a potentially successful business—to "get well"—and then to fund research to cure cancer and help others "get well" too!

Meeting Don was really not a surprise to me. He came into my life at a time when I had already proven myself, when I had had some successes and made good money, when I was looking for the next stage in my life plan. I had even asked for a mentor, a helper, a supporter to show up—and there came Don with his "get well" message.

My homework from that first meeting with Don was to go away and put down on paper what I needed to get well. Don asked me to take some private time for myself to think about the concept of getting well and what that would mean to me. I started thinking and jotting down ideas right away. I was completely locked in on this concept of getting well. I had seen how this had worked in my personal finances with my husband when we became debt free. We had worked together to get well in our basic financial status after some early struggles with credit card bills, auto loans, and a lack of communication about those outstanding things in our relationship. We "got well" through a process of changing our approach to money and bills as a married couple. Once we got on the same page and started going in the same direction together, the bills got paid, the debt was gone, and our relationship improved immensely on a fundamental level.

But what Don was suggesting was even bigger than all that. I could understand the parallels here. Once I could identify what it was that I thought would make me "get well," a plan could be made and steps could be taken so I could truly "get well," which would lead me ultimately to my goal to fund research to cure cancer. Simple, right?

1. What is on your bucket list?
2. Does it feel complete?

Chapter Thirteen

An Overview of the Get Well Plan

AS I TELL THIS PART OF MY STORY ABOUT THE Get Well Plan, I know your mind must be turning. You may be thinking about setting up your own Get Well Plan. Well, great!!! That is what I was hoping you would want to do. I will continue with my story about Don and how he taught me about the Get Well Plan, but before I do that, you may want to spend a little time here to get started and pursue your own plan. I will do my best to help you with that process and make it "just right" for your needs, based on what Don taught me.

Consider what you'd like to include in your own Get Well Plan.

So let's consider what you'd like to include in your own Get Well Plan. The first step is to get out a piece of paper and a pen or pencil. Now, jot down anything that comes to mind that means something to you as it relates to getting well. It could be related to your health. Or possibly your personal relationships, your family, or your job. If you are looking to have more stuff, write that down too. You want to capture the things that matter to you on a physical, spiritual, and emotional level.

Once you have captured everything you can think of right now, next put a monetary value on the material items and maybe a timeline for both the monetary and non-monetary ideas you have listed. If you want to go to Spain, for instance, you may want to put down both the cost and the timing. In this example, they are equally important to consider. Be free with this process and put down EVERYTHING, no matter how crazy your mind thinks it is.

I suggest that you list all of your dreams on the left side of your paper and the costs and timelines on the right side. This is your Get Well Plan.

If you want to go to the moon, put it down. Anything is possible. You want to be free thinking and open to what your heart desires. Your dreams can be both personal and professional.

I suggest that you list all of your dreams on the left side of your paper and the costs and timelines on the right side. **This is your Get Well Plan.** It is that simple and it is powerful. You will want to keep this in a place where you will see it often. You will also want to review it from time to time. Your Get Well Plan is important to you because it represents your heart's desires and your dreams. It is a paper representation of all that you want to have come true in your life. This is your list to sustainable abundance. It should contain everything, including all of the wishes that you believe will feed your soul. You will know when your list is finished, when you have included everything. You will feel "complete." So, be free with your dreams and don't hold anything back.

After you've recorded everything, including the associated costs and time frames, what is next? Action, that's what! I had the opportunity to work with Don over a number of years on my Get Well Plan, and I have documented that process here for you in the next few chapters. The key part of Don's advice to me was not how to acquire the things on my Get Well Plan, rather it was doing the best I could in life, while holding the knowledge that I am a creator and that I have choices and abundance available to me at all times. Over time, things started to get done on that list.

I had the great fortune of seeing many of my life's goals and dreams come to fruition. I was able to experience the Get Well Plan in action for my benefit and the benefit of my business, family, and friends. I saw how things came to be. Just like when I had paid off all of my bills in the five-step program, my Get Well Plan was coming true. The momentum was in place. Each year, I was able to see progress and I was able to remove things off my Get Well Plan because I had accomplished them. My relationship with my husband was great, my relationship with my own body was great, and spiritually, I was connecting more and more to my inner self and to God. Life really was good, and I was ever closer to sustainable abundance. I was fortunate to have a mentor like Don to keep me on track. I realize now as I look back that having that initial plan was the beginning of a great process of achievement for me.

Almost like getting your doctorate, you set your sights on the topic and then work toward it for years until you get it done. This is similar. Although there is not a school for the Get Well Plan, this plan is something that you ultimately must do for yourself. It certainly helps to have your partner and your family on board for this process and to surround yourself with other people who are of the same mindset.

One of my current habits is to review the Get Well Plan at the end of each year and see where I have come in that year. I am able to track my progress there on that sheet from my original Get Well Plan and make revisions as needed. My husband has started his own Get Well Plan, too, so we now compare notes and support each other in any way we can.

But before I get too far ahead of myself, let's continue the story of Don and how he helped me launch my Get Well Plan off to a great start. Let's see if you can glean some useful tips from my experience as I continue to share it with you.

1. How do you see your life in three years? How about in five years?
2. If now is not the time to begin dreaming, when will be the right time?

Chapter Fourteen

Next Steps to Making a Get Well Plan

DO YOU HAVE A PLACE THAT YOU LIKE TO GO when you really need to think? A place away from work, the kids, traffic, phones, and other distractions? I learned to extract myself from everyday life when I needed time to focus. When I met Don, I was at one of those junctures.

It was time to take action. I was turned on by this idea that I could have what I wanted, that I deserved it, and that it was okay to want more for myself and for my family. I was motivated and ready to go. I decided to spend some quality time on my "get well" list and went to my favorite library at a local university. I spent about three hours there working on my "get well" thoughts and ideas as well as on my business plan. The library was the perfect place for this because no phones are allowed and it is quiet enough to think and write uninterrupted. There was space to create, which was exactly what I wanted. I wanted the time and the space to create and envision my future.

I started out with my "get well" list looking at everything from a financial point of view. *What if we had the mortgage paid for? That would certainly take some strain off my mind and body. If our mortgage payment went away, then our monthly financial obligations would change drastically without the demands of that payment. I would be less stressed and feel freer to do more towards my goal of curing cancer. The direction of my energies could shift.*

I started to understand more about what this "get well" concept could mean for me. I felt expanded and free just thinking about the possibilities it offered. I got motivated. I wanted to further explore this plan of how I could get well, of what it would mean for me to get well and what it would take to remove all those things that made me work so hard every day to try and meet those needs.

I threw abandon to the wind and started to expand on my "get well" list. I already shared with you my monetized list. Here's what my preliminary list looked like:

1. Pay off home mortgage
2. Get my dream car
3. Fund my retirement
4. Buy a mountain retreat
5. Slush fund for home maintenance
6. Garages for cars

These were my initial personal monetary goals for getting well. I envisioned my life with all of these things in place, paid for and working in my life. My list continued on with a focus on quality of life, because I knew to truly "get well" I would need a healthier lifestyle to go along with my financial health.

So, here is how my "get well" list continued:

1. CURE CANCER
2. Balance in my life—time at home with my husband, family, and friends
3. Respect and honor myself
4. Reach my full potential
5. Create
6. Be around good people with motivations like me to help others
7. Find a mentor to guide and support me as I reach my full potential
8. Have FUN and enjoy this great process of getting well, because it is so exciting to have a plan to "Get Well"
9. Give back and share this magic with others

AND once I "get well" in these areas of finance and my personal life, as well as in my business, I can GIVE like I have never given before. My dreams of curing cancer are just a part of that. My mind, heart, and soul were on fire with this whole idea of how I could "get well" and what I could do for myself and others once I did!

$ $ $

Well, now I had all this fire in my belly and a list of things I wanted to accomplish, but, of course, reality then set in. The questions, the doubting, and the anxiety kicked in. *How the heck am I going to "get well" and do all of this?*

This guy Don, whom I'd met once, had turned on this machine, given me the concept, and told me to do the homework. *But...now what?* He had offered to give me a day of his time, which I later learned was a privilege to be offered. Deep inside, I knew he was solid and held the key to the rest of the process. I just needed to act and receive his help.

I realized I needed to book that "get well" day for myself with Don, and I started the process to make the arrangements. Since he was in such high demand, I learned that finding a full day on his calendar was a rarity. He made it work, though, and we found a date and set it.

Chapter Fifteen

The Process and How It Works

JUST FOUR WEEKS AFTER OUR FIRST MEETING, Don and I had our "Get Well Day." I arrived in Orlando on a cross-country flight late the night before our scheduled meeting. He didn't want any payment for what he was doing for me. He just wanted to see me "get well" so I could get on with my ultimate goal to cure cancer.

I knew that our first meeting at that conference had not been by chance. It was meant to be. It was grace. It was the Great Spirit at work. I recognized the significance of our encounter when I met Don and listened to him talk about his own life and why he was motivated to do what he did to help others. I saw myself in him. I wanted to be like him—WELL. The timing was perfect for him to show up when he did, and I'm sure if you ask others he has helped to get well, they would tell you the same thing.

Don didn't tell me much about what would happen during our day together, but he did send me a list of things he needed from me before we met. They included the following:

- any financials I had
- an NDA
- any business plans
- any company literature
- any marketing materials
- other appropriate materials—letters of commendation, letters requesting business relationships

I scrambled to put things together a few days before my trip. I'm embarrassed to say I had to look up "NDA" on the Internet, which was a Non-Disclosure Agreement. Aha! *Savvy guy*, I thought. I had a lot yet to learn! He <u>was</u> watching out for my best interests and making sure that our information stayed confidential. *Thank you, validation.*

Another embarrassment was that my business plan had been written by hand. I had not taken the time to complete a formal business plan for my own business. I copied it anyway and sent it. I found an NDA online, filled it out, and sent it along as well. My financials were in great shape, thanks to my bookkeepers and accountants who worked with me to get them together. I was light on the marketing materials and had one letter I thought was of value to send ahead—a letter I'd received from a businessman who had approached me about doing a venture with me.

The following entry is straight out of my diaries that I kept from the first few meetings I had with Don. I kept a diary so that someday I would be able to look back and say, "Wow, that *Get Well Program* thing really worked!" Well, today is that day, so I am sharing this secret to success with you.

$$$

December 4, 2006. I felt anxiety about coming to Orlando to meet Don. Heck, I had only met the guy once before in Dubai at one of my conferences. But something told me this guy was different, unique, and trustworthy, even without knowing him very long. A trusted friend introduced us to each other and actually sat in on that very first meeting.

I was nervous, I admit. *What was going to happen, and where would the day lead? What would my "Get Well" process look like after this? Would I know the answers to how I would be able to "Get Well"? And who was this guy—really?*

Don was scheduled to pick me up at 8:30 in the morning, and we planned to go to a law office nearby and use one of their conference rooms throughout the day. He had scheduled a lunch meeting with two attorneys and was taking me to dinner—at least I knew I was going to be well fed! Other than that, I didn't have a clue about what to expect.

Don arrived on time and off we went to the law firm. It was a relief to see him again and to hear his deep, radio broadcast voice. It wasn't long before he mentioned that we were going to be talking that day about "getting well." I knew this was going to turn into an interesting day, and he knew exactly how the process was going to play out.

I noticed when we exited the car in the parking garage that Don picked up a framed picture from the backseat and carried it under his arm as we headed for the building elevators. Soon enough, I learned what it portrayed.

Don greeted everyone we met. He spoke to the ladies in the elevator, commenting on the day. I noticed how he attracted them to somehow open up so that they were soon laughing and smiling and enjoying themselves. He had a special way of treating people and acknowledging each one individually. In turn, they responded to him positively. When we reached the office, it was obvious that they knew him well and were happy to see him. His behavior made me question how I interact with others—*am I that kind and respectful of others? Not enough, but I could be. And look at the reaction I could receive.*

Don was swimming with the whales, close to the surface, maybe fifteen feet underwater and right next to an 80,000-pound momma whale.

We settled into the conference room, and Don started out by presenting the framed picture. He held it up to reveal a beautiful photograph of a mother whale with her baby swimming by her side—in the ocean along with DON! Yes, Don was swimming with the whales, close to the surface, maybe fifteen feet underwater and right next to an 80,000-pound momma whale. The picture was just a year old, and as he told me the details of how the photograph came about, I recognized once again that he was not your ordinary, regular guy—*and yet he was.* "Nature is bigger than us, and we are a part of nature too," he said. "It's a beautiful thing. Keep this picture in your mind as we go through this day. Now it's time to talk about getting well. Did I mention that before?"

Don asked me questions and I answered. I felt as though I was losing my footing. I was uncertain of my direction and goals. I found my brain trying to grasp reality—to rationalize. I was also thinking creatively for the first time in a while. I found I had someone to talk with, someone who challenged me, someone I felt safe with, and someone who had great resources (and I was about to find out just HOW great).

Before I knew it, we were joined by a young woman whom Don had invited to come and meet me. She owned her own PR firm and obviously had been where I was at some prior point in time. Don asked her to tell me a little bit about herself and her background. She told me about her former career in television media and subsequent work with the city mayor's office. Then she said that she had decided she wanted more time with her son and a different quality of life. She wanted to "get well," she added. Don nodded. So, she quit her job and started her own business and was doing great.

Then Don asked me to introduce myself and talk about my goals to "get well." I felt as if I had just joined a club. It was as if we had a new kind of shorthand going on between us because we knew what "get well" meant. The conversation was open and turned into a brainstorming session between the three of us. Her input gave me new concepts to consider and made me open some creative doors for myself.

Time was going by much too quickly. Already it was time for our lunch meeting. We headed back to the hotel to sit down with two of Don's friends who were very high-powered attorneys and businessmen. I had stopped trying to figure out what the process was going to be and just became more and more open and receptive. It was a seemingly free flow of energy and synergies, yet Don was orchestrating it every step of the way. Each person was a set-up. Even if I didn't understand it in the moment, but there was a purpose and a reason why I was meeting them all. I began to understand that Don knew them all and had put them together with me for a reason. And because it was Don who called them and set up the meetings, they came. They trusted him impeccably and knew this would be worthwhile for them, that it would not be a waste of their time because Don had set it up.

When Don asked me to tell them about myself, I felt a renewed energy within. I did not feel weird telling these people that I wanted to get well so I could do well—and what my reasons were for doing so. Talking about my daughter had been hard for me to do in business settings up until then. I felt infused with a sense of confidence I had never before experienced. And when the term "get well" came up again, I knew I was being further inducted into the club. These guys were already members and very "well." Don was showing me how it looked to "get well" and then offer help to others. I was getting the opportunity throughout this day to see examples of people who were in the Get Well Club, and I was proud to be a part of it.

Internally, I was getting it on an even deeper level. *Don was giving me a "get well" network and setting me up to succeed!* There were some gems uncovered at lunch from a business standpoint, but more importantly, I was gaining a deeper understanding of the "get well" process, and I was happy.

We returned to the law office's conference room and started back to work. I was surprised that we never talked specifically about all the items Don asked me to send him, but it was apparent he had looked at them and used everything I'd provided to formulate my process. He started to make phone calls on speaker phone, reaching out to more Get Well Club members.

He put me in touch via phone with Phil, another "get well" member who had started his own company. Phil was a professional journalist who had left his stellar career to get a life and "get well." He worked on marketing brochures, marketing plans, and business plans. Here was a guy who could help me get my package together, including my business plan, and he was reasonably priced.

We spoke to numerous other contacts, each of them hand-selected to help me "get well." Each one represented a piece of the puzzle I needed, and each one was a member of the Get Well Club. Each had a purpose and a reason for getting well themselves and each wanted to help others. My brain was about to explode, but my adrenalin was simultaneously rushing full bore. I knew there was no time for stopping yet.

Don took me back to the hotel and dropped me off, providing me with a much-needed break. He told me he would be back to pick me up for dinner. I went to my room but found I couldn't relax. I was so hyper from all of the day's activities, and I was processing it all, trying to sort, prioritize, realize, and relax. It was pretty overwhelming, and I knew that I could not or should not expect all of the ideas we'd talked about that day to be accomplished by me alone. I would need help, guidance, and support. Don was giving me that—he was building it for me. He was setting me up to "get well." Did I mention that before?

The evening drive to dinner included a phone call to another connection for me. Don seemed tireless in his efforts to put me in contact with people who were seemingly good matches for me and my goals. Throughout our time together that day, it was apparent that he had grasped the gist of what I did and understood my desires to move forward. He was obviously in his element and had been doing this type of thing all his life, because he had an unending list of contacts he was willing to share. He was right in there with me, bringing me out of my shell, helping me brainstorm, finding others for me to brainstorm with—others who would help me reach my goals.

As we drove, I thought back on Don and the day we'd shared so far. He was a miracle put right in front of me, and had I not been receptive I could have missed it! Who would have believed that someone so genuine would come along and open up their rolodex, offer their time, and help someone else achieve their goals? Who could have imagined that there might be someone willing to teach another how to "get well" without having a sales pitch, hidden agenda, or ulterior motive? It was hard to believe, but I was glad I had not allowed my skepticism to stop me from following through to meet with Don. God gave me a gift in Don, and Don showed me how I wanted to be. I saw Don having the time of his life as he helped me out and interacted with others like me. I wanted to be there, and I realized that I wanted to be like him—I wanted to give back too.

Well, Don and I had dinner and talked about the day and ourselves. He and I both drew doodles on a notepad—something we had in common—diagrams. We discussed more about content—my business plan, getting an advisory board, how to prioritize twenty-four hours in a day, and how to enjoy quality of life in the midst of my business endeavors. *How full is your plate? How full should it be?* How full do you want it to be? These were all questions we explored together.

With the way the day had gone, I felt like I was in a movie script or book. Then I discovered that it wasn't over yet. After Don dropped me back at the hotel, he called about 10:00 p.m. and asked if I had time to talk to someone else. He then introduced me to another of his connections—another Get Well Club member. This one was a genius match that only I would understand because of another business opportunity that had been offered to me separate from Don's group.

As I created the scenario in my head and we talked about possible ideas, I could see that making a priority list for me was key. This was an opportunity to set up something that would "sell while you sleep," which was

Don's terminology. This was another step in the process of getting well—finding things that would generate positive cash flow so you could sit back and "get well."

Well, my day was done, but the lessons were just beginning. I knew that my next steps with Don would be formative, so I dozed off into a dream world of getting well in order to face another day with renewed energy.

$$\$\,\$\,\$$

Don and I continued to talk on the phone and meet in person about four times a year. I asked him to sit on my advisory board as the chair, which he did. Over time, we built an incredible friendship that was as close to family as one could get. Don's contacts have become friends too and many of the people I met that first day are still in contact with me. What Don gave me with his attention towards my business and activities was unprecedented access to his network. I brought along my willingness to work and relate to people and also to learn as much as possible about doing business and deals. We became involved in numerous projects around the world and supported each other with our contacts and expertise as much as possible.

Don helped me through some crisis events in my business too. He was always willing to lend a helping hand. He believed in me and my success, like he did his other members of the "Get Well Club." We have all benefited from working together and knowing each other. Don's primary criterion was a person's character, so we all knew that when we met one of Don's contacts, they were people of integrity and good character. It has been a fun way to work.

Don's concept of the Get Well Plan has become a part of my normal dialogue and life. I have accomplished a great deal by going for it and knowing what I was aiming for. Over the years I have been doing the Get Well Plan, I have reviewed it each year to see what progress I have made, added some new dreams that I've come up with along the way, and taken off those that I reached or that I changed my mind about. The bottom line is that I am so much closer than ever before to having my life look and be the way that I always dreamed. My husband and I have afforded wonderful trips together and enjoy a much more balanced and loving life together because of this effort to put our dreams on paper and share it with each other. He has dreams too. And many of them have come true as well.

By now, I hope you know the secrets behind the Get Well Plan and can see how simple it really is. If you have not already done so, take time now to write down what you have been dreaming of for your long-term future. Use the form on the following pages to record all of your dreams. You can believe in yourself and allow your dreams to come true.

Your Get Well Plan

MAKE A LIST HERE OF WHAT YOU WANT IN your life. Include tangible and non-tangible things. Include the goals, dreams, experiences, and assets you want in your life.

LIST OF ITEMS   EST. VALUE

Financial List:

_____ $_____

_____ $_____

_____ $_____

_____ $_____

_____ $_____

_____ $_____

_____ $_____

_____ $_____

_____ $_____

_____ $_____

Sub-Total $_____

Emotional/Mental List:

_____ $_____

_____ $_____

_____ $_____

_____ $_____

_____ $_____

_____ $_____

_____ $_____

_____ $_____

_____ $_____

_____ $_____

Sub-Total $_____

Physical List:

_____ $_____

_____ $_____

_____ $_____

_____ $_____

_____ $_____

_____ $_____

_____ $_____

_____ $_____

_____ $_____

_____ $_____

Sub-Total $_____

Experiences List:

_____	$_____
_____	$_____
_____	$_____
_____	$_____
_____	$_____
_____	$_____
_____	$_____
_____	$_____
_____	$_____
_____	$_____

Sub-Total $_____

Spiritual List:

_____	$_____
_____	$_____
_____	$_____
_____	$_____
_____	$_____
_____	$_____
_____	$_____
_____	$_____
_____	$_____
_____	$_____

Sub-Total $_____

Giving List:

_____	$_____
_____	$_____
_____	$_____
_____	$_____
_____	$_____
_____	$_____
_____	$_____
_____	$_____
_____	$_____
_____	$_____

Sub-Total $_____

Other:

_____	$_____
_____	$_____
_____	$_____
_____	$_____
_____	$_____
_____	$_____
_____	$_____
_____	$_____
_____	$_____
_____	$_____

Sub-Total $_____

TOTAL: $_____

PART FIVE

*How to Break Through
the Obstacles to Personal Wellbeing*

Chapter Sixteen

Some Misunderstandings About Money

I WAS RAISED TO SAVE UP MY MONEY TO pay for what I wanted—clothes, a car, private school, an apartment—and eventually to support myself. Later, when I entered the financial industry, the advice from most financial experts was to use OPM (Other People's Money) to get whatever we wanted or desired. Back in the '80s and '90s, the credit card was becoming more prevalent and more available to everyone in America. This did not happen overnight, but over time. The banks recognized the potential of revenues they would reach by offering credit to every working adult. As more women came into the work force, and not only became earners but also primary spenders in families, credit cards became easier for them to obtain as well. Leverage and debt were becoming a way of life for all of us—our new NORM in the USA.

Even college students became targets for the credit card issuers. Offers were open to students on campuses across the nation, whether or not they were currently earning income. People were no longer earning their money and then spending it when they had enough in their accounts. We were not using cash to buy things; rather, we began to pull out that credit card and grow debt in our households. And we no longer had to have the income to justify the line of credit amounts the credit card companies offered. We were leveraging everything, even food and gas on credit cards.

As a nation, we were living under a false sense of security, convincing ourselves that we would be able to pay off our debts—no problem. We believed the credit card companies when they sent us new applications in the mail and said we had qualified for a new $10,000 limit. We used our home equity to buy more stuff and upgrade our lifestyles. We created a bubble of credit, the likes of which had never been seen in this country before. This credit and borrowing norm came back to bite us in 2008 when the peak of leverage and sub-prime lending crashed the banks and then the markets. We learned the hard way that having all that credit is not necessarily the way to build personal wealth.

We created a bubble of credit, the likes of which had never been seen in this country before.

I have met with several individuals who were leveraged to the hilt when everything fell apart. One friend of mine lost nine rental properties and had to file bankruptcy because they had leveraged everything. In fact, it turns out that many Americans lost everything when the financial crisis hit. They were just one paycheck away from disaster, and when disaster hit they were caught in the downturn.

Subsequently, many Americans have turned away from living on credit or they have been forced to live on what they earn because they no longer can get credit. If we all were to balance our own expenses and incomes, I believe the country would be in a better place economically. This may be a movement underway, because I heard recently that just over 30% of Americans now have paid off their home mortgages. I also have heard that many more young people are now living a more conservative lifestyle and postponing marriage or buying a home so they can save up enough money first.

My husband and I were already on the road to recovery from debt when the markets crashed in 2008. We had paid off our mortgage, had money in the bank, and held no debt. I remember being extremely relieved that we were not going to lose our home or cars. Maybe even more importantly, neither of us was going to lose sleep at night over money. It was stressful enough to watch or listen to the news each night as they talked about the economy and people losing their homes and jobs. It was a truly scary time. This is why I also want to encourage you to look at your own situation now and start or continue to live debt free. It will change your life.

So, let's take a look at some of the misunderstandings about money.

1. **OPM—Other People's Money.** Like I explained above, this is one of the oldest adages of the 20th century. Let's drop this one and shift it to LWYM—Live Within Your Means!

2. **Credit scores.** Do you know what your credit score is? Do you care? You probably do care because you have been told that you need a high credit score in order to qualify for MORE CREDIT—and because you have been told that you need to have a credit score to qualify for a mortgage in order to buy a house or a car. Credit scores are a means to get you to borrow more money and use more credit. This makes no sense. You have to borrow money and make timely payments in order to get a high score so you can borrow more money. In my opinion, this is ludicrous. I don't have a credit score because I don't owe any money. I don't need a credit score because I don't buy anything I cannot afford to buy outright—including cars, homes, clothes, food, and gas. Rethink your reasons for wanting a credit score. Consider how you can better use your money for your own benefit and not for the benefit of the lender who is making money off of your interest payments. Save that interest for yourself and use it for your own future.

3. **Lease vs. own.** I am referring to car leases here. When I first met my husband, he was leasing his car. Even back then, I was against having to pay for a car via a car payment, but leasing a car made even less sense to me. I could not figure out why he was paying a bank each month to drive a car he would never own, yet

had to insure, fill with gas, and limit his miles, just to turn it back into the dealer three years later with nothing to show for it. I convinced him to buy the car and never lease again. Even if we had to buy a clunker with cash, at least we would not have a payment and lose all that money to interest payments. Cars become outrageously expensive when you do the math and figure out how much you are paying for them over the time of a loan. Don't ever lease a car, and if you have a lease now, find out what it would cost you to buy it out and get yourself off the lease. Then, go buy what you can afford and trade up when you can. Used cars are a much better deal than new, once you figure in the depreciation of a new car when you drive it off the lot. There are plenty of gently used cars available to meet anyone's needs. I have also used a car broker to help me buy and sell cars. They take a commission, which is built into the price of the car, but they do all the haggling and bring the cars to me for test drives. I can buy or sell a car without ever having to go to the dealership. I know many of you like the haggling part of buying a car, but if you don't, a reliable car broker is a great option.

4. **0% interest.** When you hear 0% interest, do you think this means free? Well, guess what? Nothing is free in this world, so you are paying somewhere. There is always a place somewhere in that deal where the lender is making money off of you. If it is a 0% loan, then you are paying a built-in fee somewhere, or a higher price for the item. There may even be a clause where the initial interest is 0% and then it changes.

Never trust a loan advertisement that claims to be without some way of charging you for using OPM. They always will get their pound of flesh from you, the borrower.

5. **No Money Down.** Yes, it is true. You can buy things with no money down. Cars, houses, furniture, boats, and lots of other stuff. Again, you will pay on the other end. Your interest rates will be higher or the length of the loan will be longer. You will always pay more for these kinds of offers. They are still loans and should be avoided at all costs.

6. **Lower your interest rate at no cost to you.** With interest rates dropping to record rates, mortgage lenders are looking for more homeowners to refinance their mortgages. One way to do this is by paying for your closing costs and making it so you have no out-of-pocket costs to redo your loans. Be careful in this arena. My son recently asked me about an offer that his mortgage lender offered him under these terms. When we sat down and did the math, he would have been paying a substantial amount over time to pay for that refinance. We did some more homework and found a shorter term loan—a fifteen-year that would be more beneficial to him in the long run, even with the loan refinance fees incorporated in the new loan. Shop around for this and be sure to do the homework with the numbers and terms so you know what you are paying for and if it will actually save you money in the long run or if you should pass and look at ways to pay down your mortgage faster.

7. **Cash is dangerous to carry.** Have you ever thought about what your downside risk would be if you lost your cash or were robbed of your cash versus your credit cards? I look at it this way—if I lose my cash that is all I lose. If I were to lose a credit card, then my risk is whatever the credit limit is on that card and all the other cards I might have in my wallet. *Ouch.* I carry cash to pay for food and incidentals, so I am not using a card (I only use debit cards now) for those purchases. As I expressed much earlier, I also find that it is harder and more painful when you are paying cash for things. If you have not done this in a while, you will find it very instructive. I learned that I was able to think more about what I was buying when I paid cash for it. And I look for better deals when I am paying cash. I am less likely to pay full price for anything when I pay cash. And I am limited in what I can spend, because if I don't have the money in my wallet then I cannot buy the item. If I go home and still want that item, then I will take more cash out of my stash at home and go back and make the purchase. Most often, though, if I walk away and think about it, I either don't need it or don't want to spend the money on it after all. I am a compulsive buyer, so having to limit my purchases with the cash I have allotted myself each month has curbed my spending many times over. And I have what I want and definitely more than I need.

These are just some of the more obvious misunderstandings about money. What I would suggest is that you stop and think about these things and really put yourself and your money in first place instead of the banks, credit cards, or shopping malls. Think about what other misunderstandings you might hold that keep you from being in first position. No matter what misconceptions you might have held, remember that you are the consumer and "they" are trying to get you to spend your money on stuff wherever you are, whether you need it or not.

We have very few places in our lives now that we are not being marketed to—through the Internet, our smartphones, online, in the grocery store, via our car radio, and of course, on television. To be aware of these marketing ploys and what we really need or want comes down to discipline of our earnings. Using our budgets and cash as tools to manage our money and know where our money goes is the way to take care of ourselves and stay out of financial trouble. I am all for spending money—it is really fun. I encourage you to enjoy your money and spend it when you have it—then there is no credit hangover. It is a great way to live, and I want you to try it for yourself.

Remember, if your money has a name, then it knows where to go. And this does not mean you cannot have what you want; it means that you buy what you want for yourself on your own terms, not on a bank's terms. You want to save those premiums and interest payments for your own benefit instead of for the bank's. Be smart with your money and you will have enough to take care of yourself … and then some.

1. Do any of these misunderstandings sound familiar to you?
2. If so, what have you learned that might change your attitudes towards these beliefs?
3. Are you willing to change some of your beliefs about money?

Chapter Seventeen

Money Can't Buy You Love

DO YOU KNOW THE BEATLES SONG "CAN'T Buy ME Love"? Simple words, but oh, so true. More marriages and relationships fail because of money issues than for almost any other reason. Money is hard to talk about for most people. It has a lot of power over us if we let it. I am here to tell you, once you get your money conversation truly in the open with your partner, the rest of life and your relationship will get a lot easier. Open communication about money is key to a healthy relationship. So, when you sit down to write out your Get Well Plan, include your partner, spouse, and children. This is your chance to talk about your dreams and to learn about what the other person's dreams are too. This is about building trust—about sharing bank accounts, investments, and asset building. All of these things are based on trust. Trust that you will be together now and in the future.

If you are a single person and doing this on your own, I suggest that you identify someone in your life, either a family member or close friend, with whom you can discuss money issues. Ask them to help you with your plan and keep you on track. You want to be careful here, though, as you decide who to choose. You need to know whether or not they have a different philosophy than you when it comes to money. For instance, if you are eliminating debt and doing this plan, then you need to be working with someone else who is on the same track. You can do it together and hold each other accountable as you go through your processes. Set up meetings with each other to go over your budgets. I did this with my son. We met the first part of each month and went over budgets and his Get Well Plan to keep on track. It has been great to have that connection with him and to watch him take on more responsibility as he learns more about his own money and how to make it work for him. And I do this with clients when I work with them as a financial coach.

Many relationships have yielded bad outcomes both emotionally and financially; so if you are one of those people who have had a bad experience financially with a former partner, this is your chance to do it differently. Finding someone who is willing to share their shortfalls along with their dreams with you is a key element to a successful relationship and a real growth experience. Often we don't want the other person to know that we have debt or can't pay our bills. We attempt to keep up an image that is good on the outside but stinks on the inside. That false image will not help you create and live your plan.

When is the right time to talk about money? Probably not on the first date! But if you are in a serious relationship, talking about your money and theirs is imperative. I know this is a hard subject to broach, but I encourage you to be brave and lay it all out on the table with each other. If you cannot deal with money together before you are married or committed for the long term, statistics show you most likely won't succeed as a couple. Money can't buy you love, but it can sure wreak a lot of havoc in your love life.

Working through issues, including money issues, is part of building a life together and experiencing your accomplishments with each other. It's one of the most rewarding or painful things couples can go through—building their lives and fulfilling their dreams, each one, together.

Be sure to include each other in the process. One of you will most likely be better at the bookwork than the other, but it's really important that you both sit down **My husband says, "Every couple needs a nerd, and honey, you're it!"** together to do the budget, pay bills, and write out the Get Well Plan. My husband says, "Every couple needs a nerd, and honey, you're it!" As I said before, I am the financial nerd, but I make sure to include my husband in financial matters, discussions, and decisions—at home and in my business. His perspective and input are invaluable to our success as a couple. If I don't have his buy-in, then I am not in alignment with him, which ultimately causes friction and leaves him unhappy. The same applies in reverse. We both respect and love one another enough to include each other in our lives completely, including matters that involve our money.

A note about managing your accounts: putting your money together can be a scary thing. Again, it comes down to trust. My husband and I were both married before, so we came to our relationship with major trust issues when it came to money. We were one of those couples that had bad financial experiences with former partners. So, we decided to maintain our own individual accounts and open a joint account for household expenses, savings, and "just in case" funds. We have individual retirement accounts and business accounts. We are both signers and beneficiaries on each other's accounts and have access to statements, passwords, safe deposit boxes, and so on. There is transparency in our financial lives with each other now, and we both know where everything is held. We manage our own equity holdings because of my background as a financial representative, but we also have a friend who is an advisor to my husband, should he need help with decisions about our stock holdings if anything happens to me. We have set up a living trust to make sure our assets are easier to manage long after we are gone.

We have a working system that works for us.

1. What is your system?
2. What do you want it to be?
3. Can you start today to build a system that includes your relationship with your partner and your money?

Chapter Eighteen

When Trouble Comes Along ... Stuff Happens

REMEMBER THAT JUST IN CASE SAVINGS account? Yes, that stash I told you about setting aside for a rainy day? Well, I hope you never have to use that money. I hope it sits there for you forever and you never really need to use it. But "just in case" you have a water leak, a fire, or lose your job, or get sick, then you have planned for this. You have a way to take care of your problem financially. The stress and strain of an emergency does not have to include whether or not you can afford it. This Just in Case Account allows you the freedom to deal with your emergency emotionally and practically. You need to spend your energy on getting better or getting things back to working order, whatever the case may be. We can never predict what our disruptions will be in life, only that we will have them.

The magic of having a Just in Case Savings Account is that once you have one you may find that you rarely need to use it. For me and my husband, anytime we have an emergency come up now, we look anywhere else we can to find the money to pay for it before we go to the Just in Case fund. Occasionally, though, we have had to tap into it. When that has happened, we've replaced the money in that account as quickly as we could. One time, our basement flooded from a broken water heater and we needed to replace it immediately. I had to write the check for the new water heater on the spot. Luckily we had the Just in Case Account fully funded, and our emergency did not then turn into a financial burden as well.

We can never predict what our disruptions will be in life, only that we will have them.

In early 2013, my husband needed knee surgery. He wanted to go out of network to a specialist and that meant money out of our pockets to pay the big deductible. We scraped together as much money as we could from miscellaneous accounts and then tapped into the Just in Case Account for the rest. We were fortunate to have the option for him to get his surgery done by a specialist and not be put in a financial bind because of that choice. We were able to afford it and keep on going. He has fully recovered now, and we have since replaced the funds to our Just in Case Account.

Like I said, once you have this account in place and funded, you most likely will not need to use it. But, it is nice to have that peace of mind when you do have it in place and you are able to take care of any emergency that comes along unexpectedly.

1. Are you ready for the unexpected?
2. Do you have that money set aside to take care of emergencies?
3. How can you take care of yourself and make sure you have what you need?

Chapter Nineteen

There is Enough (But ... How Much is Enough?)

YOU MAY HAVE HEARD—THERE IS ENOUGH for all of us. Have you ever asked yourself, though, what is enough for you? Enough for you to be happy, comfortable, taken care of, set for retirement, for your children to get a college education, and enough to take care of your dreams?

One of the primary purposes of completing your own Get Well Plan is to cause you to contemplate what your ENOUGH is. It is not to set limitations on you. Rather, it is to set targets for you to accomplish. As you begin to acquire your goals, you may find that you want to add more to your Get Well Plan. Or you may find that something you thought was really a good idea when you wrote it on your original plan may not really fit once you have some experience with your plan.

> **As you begin to acquire your goals, you may find that you want to add more to your Get Well Plan.**

For instance, my husband and I love to ski. We both grew up in Colorado and dreamed of one day having our own place in the mountains. This was one of the first things we put on our Get Well Plan. Once we had paid off our mortgage and bought a new car, it was time to start saving and looking for a mountain condo. This was three or more years into our plan. The next step was for us to begin looking at properties with a realtor, but my husband was resistant. When we sat down and talked it out, we realized that neither of us wanted the responsibilities of owning a property in the mountains. It would mean more time for maintenance and upkeep, which would affect our flexibility. We identified that time was also valuable to us, and it was not just about the money.

When it came down to it, we figured out that owning a mountain home was not for us. Rather, being able to rent someone else's nice condo or home would be perfect. That way, we could ski in different resorts and stay in a variety of locations without the ongoing expense and hassle of ownership. So, the mountain home came off our Get Well Plan. Rather, we have a savings account set aside for ski trips and rentals during ski season.

In the years we have been working our plan, some things have been added and some removed. You may have a desire for a bigger house, more or better cars, a college education for your kids, or many other dreams and desires. Let your lifetime dreams come out and see how they work for you. Experience your Get Well Plan and work with it. You can be flexible, yet focused, on accomplishing your plan. The world is full of abundance, and you now have the keys to finding yours.

1. Are you shy with money?
2. Does money make you feel guilty?
3. Does money intimidate you?
4. Do you equate math with money?

Chapter Twenty

Timing is Everything

I AM SURE YOU HAVE HEARD THIS QUOTE. "You can have anything you want; you just cannot have everything you want." I always like to add a little bit more—"all at once." In other words, I believe I will have everything I want, just not all at once. I believe I will have my Get Well Plan—the entire thing—just not all at once. I believe it is a process, and I will get it completed. Just like the Five Steps to Financial Freedom. It took some trial and error and some time to figure out what was best for me and for my husband.

Timing for you and your plan, whether you are on the Five Steps to Financial Freedom or your Get Well Plan, is all part of the fun of working with your money. Your timing is going to vary from mine or anyone else's. Timing of markets, of jobs, houses, kids, and all of the experiences we have in our lives is something we don't always have control over. I have learned over the years, though, that having a plan has helped me to survive the good times and the bad ones too. Since I did not have a crystal ball to know what might be just around the corner, my goals and plans were a guiding tool for me.

Over time, I have learned to be accepting of what I could accomplish and what I could not. I have learned to shoot for the stars. And I have learned to be open to a different timing for things, if and when that becomes necessary. For instance, I have wanted to own a convertible Porsche for over twenty years. Until recently, I did not accomplish that goal. I moved that goal from list to list each year when I did my yearend planning. And finally, it came to fruition. Not necessarily on my timing, but on the right timing, when I could really afford it and when the right car was available for me to own.

Once my Get Well Plan is completed, I will have new and bigger goals to accomplish. I will still have a carrot out there in front to go after because that is the part about living that I enjoy. I like to have things I can aspire to. And I like to explore. Our world is changing around us so fast that there are always new things on the horizon we can look forward to having or doing. One of the items on my bucket list is to fly in outer space someday. There are reports that in less than a decade there will be commercial flights to outer space that will be within reason to buy. So, I leave myself room to grow and to keep exploring and discovering new things and experiences.

Give yourself the benefit of enjoying the process of getting what you want when it is the right time. I used to buy what I wanted compulsively. I used credit and loans and OPM. I was a credit score participant, and I cared about status and what kind of stuff I could get. Now, I can still be compulsive with my mad money each month, which fulfills that desire (using up to $250 a month), and I save up for the bigger things in life that I want to acquire. My husband and I spend time together on budgets and talk about what to take on next. We are on track for our retirement plans and are currently saving for his retirement car. He says he wants one more "nice" car for his retirement, so we will continue to put aside money for that car over the next few years. He will be able to buy that car with cash when the time comes.

Earnings + time = money to buy what you want.

We are living in the new paradigm (which is really old school) of saving up for what few wants we have and using time to help us get there. *Earnings + time = money to buy what you want.* Also, time is on our side for our retirement. We have time to add to our retirement funds for another decade or more, and all that money we have set aside will be earning interest for us too. The money we have delineated for retirement will be working for us throughout that time. For the most part, we have invested those funds in solid mutual funds. Those funds will grow over time and become an even bigger nest egg for us to rely on when we stop working and earning.

1. Are you impatient?
2. Are you able to wait and watch your money grow? If not, why not?
3. Are your retirement accounts funded each year?

Chapter Twenty-One

Habits – Not the Nunnery Kind

YOU MAY BE SAYING TO YOURSELF, "THIS IS all too much! I am not sure I can get myself to a different kind of relationship with my money and feel that kind of peace of mind. It is easier to keep doing what I am doing even if I am not happy. I will make more money later on and I can pay all of this off then. The bank gives me credit and I am keeping my head above water. Plus, everyone else lives this way. How will I tell my friends I cannot go out with them because I cannot afford it or because I have a budget to live by?" I ask you to please consider making a conscious effort to let go of those old habits and replace them with better ones that support you and will give you a better outcome.

I sat down with a university student not long ago and learned that her car was in the shop. The cost of repairs was as much as it would cost to buy another used vehicle. She was tapped out and not sure what to do. She also had credit cards and student loans that were piling up. When I told her about the Five-Step Plan, she was intrigued.

We sat down and went over the basic concepts, and she was excited to learn how she could become debt free and develop a better relationship with her money. But then, as we talked more, she expressed that she did not want to give up anything at this point and she simply was not in a position to start working a five-step plan to get out of debt. She said she'd rather put the car repairs on her credit card and keep going further into debt than make any significant changes.

Does this sound familiar? The credit card companies and bankers have certainly made it easy for us to get into debt and stay there. They have made us feel good about borrowing money that we don't have and cannot afford, just to allow us to do all the things we want to do *right now*. We don't have to wait or have patience, nor do we need any discipline. This taps into basic human nature and tickles our fancy at a level that is hard to resist. It is easy to say, "Okay, I will go along with this. I can control myself and be reasonable. I will be careful." And then something breaks, or some friends call up and ask us out, or we run out of money in our checking account and need to buy gas and groceries. The next thing we know, we are using the credit cards—going further into debt and only able to pay the minimum payments on our cards.

How do I know all this? Because I am guilty of this behavior myself. Not just once or twice, but many, many times I have lived this pattern of behavior.

This is a hard cycle to break, but once you do, you will be in great shape and able to do all those things you wanted to do and have all the things you wanted to have—and be able to afford them! Now, how cool is that? Trust me, it happens all the time.

The real secret to success here is discipline. It means getting into new habits. It means taking back control of your money and making different decisions. So, when your friends call up and ask you out, you can still go. You only take a limited, budgeted amount of cash with you, however, and maybe you suggest a less expensive place to eat, or you search for coupons online for a special deal at your favorite spot. When you have a limited amount of money you can spend, you only spend that amount or less. This is a great reason to use your "Mad Money." It does not mean spoiling your fun—it means keeping within your limits when you go out to have fun.

When my kids were young and I was struggling with money, I searched for free things we could do around the city, like free days at the zoo, or touring The Mint downtown, or even going for a bike ride or a hike in the foothills. We went out to eat occasionally, but we went to fast food places that catered to kids, provided fun entertainment for them, and did not break my pocketbook. It may not have been the healthiest choice, but it was a special occasion for us and not a daily experience back then. You can find and make a list of free or inexpensive places and activities for your family to enjoy. Keep it handy on the refrigerator and schedule time to do them. You will be surprised how much fun a local adventure can be.

Be practical and start out with your first steps. Using the five simple steps outlined earlier in this book will help you achieve peace of mind about your money. It will give you more money and freedom in your life and the opportunity to pursue your dreams. Then, as you move into the next phase of your financial freedom, you will be able to see that there is another level you can reach. This is getting into the Get Well Plan.

When you begin to implement the Five-Step Plan and are paying off your debt, you are actually turning a corner in your life, helping yourself more than you might be able to see immediately. Trust me though—this is your beginning. You now have a plan for your money on a monthly basis. All of your money has a name and a place to go. It is not left up to whims or compulsive buying or even emergencies, because you have planned for everything. You have made a plan and you are now able to follow it.

Have patience with yourself and put your budget in a place that reminds you about what you are doing.

Have patience with yourself and put your budget in a place that reminds you about what you are doing. I keep mine with my ledger that I check each month when I pay bills. You may have it online and look at it when you are checking your bank account balances. Use the budget for your own advantage. It is a tool for you to follow. As I mentioned earlier, I have a cheat sheet that I make copies of for myself and my husband. Every month when we get paid, we each have a reminder of where our paycheck is going—how much to savings, money market, checking, and cash. It is all destined for a pre-assigned location. The money is following the plan, so we are in alignment with our budget. It has become a monthly habit for us, a ritual if you will.

Once you have done this a few times, it will get easier and you will develop healthy habits with your money and your budget. Good habits with money are reflective of how well you take care of other things in your life too. Deep inside, we all want to do well, and discipline is a fabulous and simple tool that allows all of us to do well in all aspects of our lives. It brings confidence and foundation to us and allows us the ability to deal with life events, both the expected and unanticipated.

1. What habits do you have that you want to keep?
2. Which ones are you ready to let go of?
3. For the ones you release, what new habits will you put in their place?
4. Are you ready to start your Five-Step Plan and write your own Get Well Plan?

Chapter Twenty-Two

Speaking of Organized

YOU WILL HELP YOURSELF A LOT IF YOU ARE organized. There are simple ways to keep track of all those papers and bills you have. I use a file cabinet drawer at home with hanging files. I keep the files pretty simple: bank statements, joint bills paid, bank receipts, auto, mortgage, income stubs, donations, cash and debit card receipts, IRA statements, investment accounts , medical, taxes for next year, and so on.

These get filed as the papers flow in and get processed.

A good time to organize is when you are doing your weekly finances. Keep it simple and make it convenient so you are able to keep up with it. If you bank online, then make desktop folders to hold your documents and keep copies

A good time to organize is when you are doing your weekly finances.

of monthly statements and payments you make. It is a good idea to keep copies of all of your statements in case something goes down or someone steals your identity. Be sure to take security precautions on your online banking. It is a good idea to have fraud insurance because it protects you and your accounts. It is not very expensive and can save you a lot of problems in the long run. As we become more of an electronic society, the risk of identity theft continues to rise, so it is important to check your accounts frequently and report any unusual charges or debits to your bank.

1. What tools do you use to set up your budgets and track your money?
2. Are you aware of where your funds are and how much you have now?
3. Do you have your budget up to date?

PART SIX

*You Now Have
Sustainable Abundance*

Chapter Twenty-Three

Doing Well and Doing Good — Take Care of Yourself so You Can Take Care of Others

SO FAR, I HAVE TALKED A LOT ABOUT HOW you can do well for yourself. One of the most rewarding things I have found with my own Get Well Plan has been my ability to share my wellbeing. It's more than just money; it's fulfillment. Once I learned how to take better care of myself financially, I was able to take care of others too. My financial wellbeing gave me the ability to give more to others without worry that I would jeopardize my own Get Well Plan.

As I shared earlier, I have found that the form of tithing works for me. In the form of a check, I give 10% of my gross pay to the organization of my choice. This is the first check I write each month. I mindfully sit down and write out the amount on the check and think about how grateful I am to be in a position to give to others. I put positive thoughts and energy into my intention to give and share every time I write a check.

I have been a giver from early days because I find true joy in sharing the wealth. I see that there will always be someone who has more than I do and someone who has less. Many people have helped me along the way by means of jobs or advice or introductions and it seems only right to pass on the giving to others. I have also had to learn my limitations and learn more about why I give. Sometimes my motivation was not in the right place, so over time I figured out what worked best for me and tweaked it to fit. I imagine that someday I will give away $1 Million, which means I will have earned $10 Million!

There is an energetic flow with money and the giving of it that I have experienced. I realize that we have great abundance in the U.S. and other developed countries, yet there are many places and people who do not share this abundance. For those of us who have more, it makes sense to give back. There's a balance to it—a goodness. And part of the Get Well Plan is to be happy and fulfilled and to feel and have that goodness in life. When we do well, we can do good for our families and friends and also for those less fortunate than we are.

Doing good isn't always just about money; it can also be about sharing your time, your experience, your wisdom, or your rolodex with someone to help them out. There's an old saying, "You can give a man a fish to feed him once or you can teach him to fish and feed him for a lifetime." Think about what you have to offer others and how you can serve.

What are you grateful for? What or who has had special meaning in your life? Look for ways to do good that match your talents. Share yourself with others, not just your pocketbook.

I told you earlier about my friend Don. He traveled the world and mentored high-level entrepreneurs and executives. He never charged for his time. He was personally well off because he had completed his own Get Well Plan years earlier, he enjoyed the business world and sharing his rolodex with others. Mostly, he liked helping others to succeed in business. He made introductions and seemed to know everyone who was anyone,

"You can give a man a fish to feed him once or you can teach him to fish and feed him for a lifetime."

no matter what line of work or what location they were in. He knew how to connect people who would benefit from knowing one another and could help each other in business. He worked with nonprofits, too, and most often if he was given compensation or stock for his efforts in a successful deal, he donated them to charities he chose to support.

One of my other mentors is an amazingly successful businessman—a billionaire in fact. Frank Giustra made his money in banking and through building businesses in mining and filmmaking. He has spent the past decade giving back. He gave over $100 Million to an initiative he started with former President Bill Clinton that creates sustainable small businesses for people in communities of underdeveloped countries. He has started an urban farming project that hires local homeless people to work the gardens and grow food in his own community of Vancouver. There are many ways he has given back and made a difference in hundreds, if not thousands, of people's lives around the world. He is a role model for me and for dozens of others he spends time with and mentors. He has done well and now he is doing a lot of good. He says if you have a nonprofit, run it like a business. Build in accountability, teach people to fish, stay results-oriented, and ask if it is really helping.

After my daughter died of cancer, I started a nonprofit organization called Dani's Foundation. The foundation raises money for cancer research but also has patient assistance and supports other families and their children who have suffered with cancer as well. One of my main goals in starting my own business was to do well so I could give more to Dani's Foundation and speed up the research process. I have donated over $300,000 to this cause through the years and have also attracted other corporate givers to the foundation. We are still working on finding a cure and have made huge progress in the effort to stop this type of cancer in young people. I feel very blessed to have been financially well enough to bring more money of my own to help fight pediatric sarcomas on behalf of my daughter, Dani, and all the others who have been affected by these cancers.

Doing business in Africa for many years has also afforded me the opportunity to help less fortunate girls in Zambia. I started a safe house, called Dani's Home, in Africa that helps girls who have been sexually abused. It was started in 2006 and houses up to sixteen girls at a time, providing them with school, a safe home to live, and medical care. Over fifty girls have been residents of Dani's Home since it opened.

These are just a few examples of what you can do when you have the means to create ways to help others. You can make things happen, and when you are open to this concept, people and circumstances will present themselves to you that will be right up your alley. You can trust that it will happen.

1. What aspirations do you have to do good?
2. Is there an organization that you would like to become more involved with financially and/or by giving your time?
3. Do you have a desire to start a nonprofit organization of your own?
4. What is the motivation to begin such an organization? Are you sure an organization similar to your vision does not already exist?
5. What will it take for you to begin your nonprofit organization?

Chapter Twenty-Four

Go Ahead – Spoil Yourself – Spend

OKAY, SO NOW WE GET TO SPEND SOME money. You have gone through a lot to get to this point. You have paid off your debt and put aside your savings for "just in case" something happens. You have been able to share some of your wealth and do some good. You have stayed on top of things and kept your focus. It seems you can breathe a little easier now. You have made it to the top of the mountain.

You have a long list of things you want to have and money in your pocket, so now you can enjoy.

The only thing to remember at this point is to stay within your means and buy with the money you have accumulated. Save up for big items like cars and houses. Save up for trips and shopping sprees. You earned it and you get to spend it.

This is where the Get Well Plan really comes into play. This is the big stuff. These are the line items that make your heart sing. You can go for the gusto. Your list of Get Well items are now your goal. You can knock them out one at a time because you have the discipline to do it. You know how this works from those early days of paying off your debts. Now you are being proactive and saving up for the things on your Get Well list. You are in control. You are your own bank and you rely on yourself to get what you want. You know how to attract more money to yourself and how to make it work for you.

You know how to attract more money to yourself and how to make it work for you.

If you want, you can now reach the place of living debt free and never having to work again. It is up to you. Now you understand the energy of money and how you relate to yours.

All of these things are within your reach—this is worth the effort you have put in. This is for you, not for a bank or any other entity. It is for you and your family to enjoy. This is living the dream—your Get Well Dream.

1. What are those line items on your Get Well list that make your heart sing?
2. Are you committed to living debt free?
3. Are you ready to save for each of those line items on your Get Well list, one at a time?
4. Are you committed to living your Get Well Dream?

Chapter Twenty-Five

You Are a Success!

NEITHER A BORROWER NOR A LENDER BE—BE an earner, a saver, a spender, and a giver, and now you know how to do all of that without borrowing or lending money.

One of my favorite sayings is, "If you fail to plan, you plan to fail."

Go back to your Get Well Plan. Revisit this every six to twelve months and track how much progress you are making. It is important to not just write out your plan but to adjust it as needed—add, accomplish, celebrate, and remove. You are getting well financially.

Now you have sustainable abundance. You have enough to relax and kick back. So, what do you want to do now? What do you want to have? Where do you want to go? Your Get Well Plan is still in place, and you are updating it as you go. It has become a part of your regular planning.

Congratulations on winning with your money. Congratulations on winning with your money. You now have the peace of mind that you dreamed of having someday. Someday is here and now. There is time to enjoy it and to do more things; you now have the financial freedom to participate.

Conclusion

I SET OUT TO WRITE A BOOK TO SHARE THE discovery of sustainable abundance in my life with you the reader. I have always wanted to help people, and I hope this book has helped you in some way to find your own solutions to your money questions. There are so many stories to tell when it comes to money and contemplating how to use it or let it take care of you. Working in the stock brokering industry taught me a tremendous amount about money and investments, but my own personal experiences have taught me even more.

The best advice I can give you is to make peace with your money. Find the discipline within yourself to live within your means and you will be more at peace. Falling into the alluring world of debt and credit does not give us peace. It makes us slaves to the lenders and creates undo worry. The magic is really a simple formula of buying what you can afford when you have the money. It is how my parents grew up and how they taught me to live from an early age.

I am thrilled to be back on track and enjoying the fruits of my labor and my good fortune. May you experience that same peace and success!

Epilogue

WHILE I WAS IN THE PROCESS OF WRITING this book my mentor, Don Mitchell, died suddenly of a heart attack. I was with him when he died—we were out to dinner and just wrapping up a business trip in Toronto. I had told him the day before he passed away that I was writing this book and that I was telling the story of our meeting and of what he had taught me about the "Get Well Plan." He just smiled and said he was looking forward to reading about it.

I am more determined than ever to share this idea with others and to mentor, assist, direct, and give to others this concept of getting well financially, physically, emotionally, and spiritually. Don was my great friend, supporter, model businessperson, and mentor. He taught me how to take care of myself, to stay balanced with my husband and work, to help others, and to do well to do good in even bigger ways than I had ever imagined. I will always hold a special place in my heart for Don, and I will aspire to be like him to others so that they too may succeed and become all that they are capable of being.

Here is an email message I sent to colleagues one week after Don's death. I want to share this with you because it epitomizes how Don lived his life and what a model he was for us, even in his passing.

March 13, 2013

Dear All,

I know the past week has been difficult for you. Don's passing was a shock for you. He had such incredible vitality and vigor. He could do more than most 40-year-olds and we thought he would be there for us and with us forever.

After having some time to think, grieve, and digest all this, I wanted to share some things with you. Don's passing was really perfectly fitting, that he left this world the way he did. I want you to know that he was gone in a flash. Don felt no pain, he was not aware of what happened, and he was happy and at peace.

Just minutes before, we had finished talking about a conference idea I had been working on in Ghana. He gave me his take on it and advised me to put it on hold for now. We were then seated at a table for two in the dining room of the restaurant and were ordering dinner when it happened. Don loved business, family, helping/mentoring people, friends, good food and wine, socializing and making a difference in people's lives. He was all of that and more when he left us.

But that is not the end of the story. Oddly, there was only one other party seated in the large dining room of the restaurant we were in last Wednesday night in Toronto. When I realized Don was in trouble, I got up to help him and one of the gentlemen from the other table came over to help me with Don. He was very helpful and gracious through the whole event. I never got his name or card because I was obviously focused on Don. Later I thought about it and realized I would never again see the man who helped me with Don that night. I was wrong.

Yesterday I received a reply to an email I sent to an oil & gas executive in Calgary, whom I had invited to present at our upcoming oil & gas conference in New York this June. I sent the email invitation to a number of company executives on February 21st of this year. Here is what his reply said:
"Michele,

I understand you were the lady to whom I helped last week with Don. If you recall I was sitting at the only other table with Ned and Bob. Sorry that was so traumatic and I was definitely affected for a while recanting the Herculean effort by the paramedics. You and I saw him taking the odd breath but he was too far gone when you and I were trying to figure out what was going on.

Small world, as Frank [another mentor of mine in Vancouver] had lunch with Bob today and explained who Don was without knowing the connection. Sorry to have met you under those circumstances.

Sincerely,

Ford "

Yes, it's true. And it is SO Don to be working his magic even in his final moments here. I'm just going to call that my first "Don Miracle." I suggest that you keep your eyes, ears, and hearts open, because I am sure there is a Don Miracle for each of you right around the corner or maybe even right in front of you now.

Bringing people together and connecting us for the greatest good of all concerned is how he lived his life. That is why we are all connected with each other. He did that. Don is with what he called "the Great Spirit" now and more powerful than ever because he is also inside each one of us. He accomplished his mission to do well and to do good by living his mantra and spreading it everywhere he went to anyone he met. Don had a Get Well Plan for us, too, and was our champion whenever we fell or achieved another milestone in our own journeys. He never liked the spotlight, but he deserved so much of the credit.

I am so grateful to have been the one chosen to be with Don at dinner that night. As I look back on it, so many things fell into alignment to make it perfect in so many ways. I still have not realized all the ways that I will miss him and mourn his loss, but my spirit is happy and knows he is fine just where he is. For each of us, we carry on for him, like he did with us. He taught us that the greatest gift we can give is ourselves, just like Don showed us and did for us.

I look forward to seeing all of you at Don's Life Celebration and know you are all in my thoughts and my heart.

With love and affection,

Michele

P.S. Please pass this on to anyone I may have missed in Don's sphere of family and friends.

About the Author

REFERRED TO AS A LINCHPIN, MS. ASHBY IS A serial entrepreneur with expertise in finance, mining, and energy. Michele Ashby, Holistic Financial Guide, started her financial career as a retail stockbroker. For twelve years, she managed over 250 client accounts and served as a mining analyst for a regional brokerage firm in Denver, Colorado. Ms. Ashby was the assistant dean for the online Mining Investment College in 1997. She has created and implemented over 100 world-renowned and private mining and energy investment forums in the U.S. and Europe, Africa, the Middle East, and Asia, designed for institutional investors, analysts, and resource companies. She has been a speaker and author in reference to stocks and financial markets for over two decades. She graduated from Regis University in Denver, Colorado with a magna cum laude degree in finance. From 1988 to 2005, Michele was founder and CEO of the Denver Gold Group, a trade association for the gold mining industry, which is now a well-known institution in the mining industry. From 2005 to July 2013, she was CEO of MiNE LLC, Meeting International Natural Resources Enterprise.

MiNE LLC was founded as a private company that organized international, private investor meetings for the finance, natural resources, mining, oil and gas, and modern energy industry sectors. MiNE LLC has produced private investor meetings globally, which featured hundreds of qualified companies and experts for institutional investors and analysts around the world. Over the years, MiNE LLC has helped foster and nurture successful business relationships with company executives and premier investment institutions.

Ms. Ashby is the author of *The Modern Energy Matchmaker*, which was released in the fall of 2010. She also published *How to Invest in Mining Stocks* in 1987.

Since 2005, Michele Ashby has been a member of the Board of Directors of McEwen Mining, (NYSE/TSX : MUX), a gold mining company with projects in North America and Mexico. She served on The Children's Hospital Oncology Advisory Board and the Board of Trustees, in Denver, Colorado, and is founder and president of Dani's Foundation. Dani's Foundation is a non-profit 501-C-3 organization founded in memory of Michele's daughter, Dani Stell, who passed away in 1999 from Ewing's Sarcoma. The foundation's mission is to find a cure and improved treatment for Ewing's Sarcoma. Michele also established Dani's Home in Livingstone, Zambia in 2007, which cares for and houses girls who have been sexually abused.

Michele is currently a financial coach for individuals and businesses, utilizing her extensive rolodex, background in finance, and networking to assist businesses and individuals. She is also facilitating productivity seminars for major Fortune 500 companies.

Michele and her husband, Keith, both Colorado natives, reside in Denver, Colorado. Michele's very colorful past include her status as a personal trainer, world-class athlete in ultra-running and indoor rowing. She enjoys reading, travel, mountain hikes, bike rides, and skiing.

Book Recommendations

THIS LIST OF BOOKS REFLECTS SOME OF MY
favorites. Each one has its own approach to work/life issues.

*The Future of Money: Creating New Wealth, Work and a Wiser
World*, Bernard Lietaer

*The Total Money Makeover: A Proven Plan for Financial
Fitness*, Dave Ramsey

48 Days to the Work You Love: Preparing for the New Normal,
Dan Miller and Dave Ramsey

*The 4-Hour Work Week: Escape 9-5, Live Anywhere, and Join
the New Rich*, Timothy Ferriss

*Take Back your Life!: Using Microsoft Office Outlook 2007 to
Get Organized and Stay Organized*, Sally McGhee

*Who Moved My Cheese?: An Amazing Way to Deal with
Change in Your Work and Your Life*, Spencer Johnson

*The Millionaire Next Door: The Surprising Secrets of America's
    Wealthy,* Thomas J. Stanley and William D. Danko
Think and Grow Rich, Napoleon Hill
God is My Partner, John Rogers with Paul Kaye

Your Forms Are Here!

Example of Budgets Worksheet –
Refer to Chapter Three

AS A STARTER, USE THIS FORM FOR YOUR simple budget. There are online budgets you can use by going to the Internet and searching for budget forms. Some of them track your expenses and income month by month and others do one monthly budget that you will need to update each month.

Remember to add in your annual expenses of insurance payments or taxes—anything you pay on a semi-annual or annual basis. Divide that amount by six or twelve months, whichever applies, and put an amount into your monthly budget. This is where you give your money a name.

You want to "spend" all of your income on this form, so write in any additional items to get you there—your "just in case" fund, mad money, and magnet money, as well as medical bills, gym dues, and other items that are not listed here but show up in your monthly expenses. If you are able to get this down on paper and review it with your family, partner, or financial helper, you are much more likely to stick to your plan and spend less, get out of debt, and save more. Good luck!

SIMPLE BUDGET

INCOME

Paycheck 1	$_____
Paycheck 2	$_____
Extra income 1	$_____
Extra income 2	$_____
TOTAL	$_____

EXPENSES

Rent/Mortgage payment	$_____
Household expenses	$_____
Food	$_____
Groceries and restaurants	$_____
Auto expenses	$_____
Loan	$_____
Gas and service	$_____

Credit card payments

Credit Card 1	$_____
Credit Card 2	$_____
Credit Card 3	$_____
Credit Card 4	$_____
Credit Card 5	$_____
Other lines of credit	$_____

Other expenses	$_____
TOTAL	$_____
Balance	$0

Example of a Cheat Sheet for Monthly Deposits of Income –
Refer to Chapter Three

I set this up at the beginning of each year and adjust it, if and when necessary. I make numerous copies and have them in a handy place to grab the first of each month on payday, so I know where all my money will go and ensure that it gets there.

Monthly Cheat Sheet
Example of a Cheat Sheet for monthly deposits of income:

John's Check

Gross Monthly Income	$4,500
Net Monthly Income	$3,192.80
Cash taken**	$1,519
Deposit checking	$1,173.80
Deposit savings	$500

** Cash breakdown for the month

Money Magnet (10%) of net	$319
Mad Money	$200
Food	$800
Gas	$200

Your Cheat Sheet:

Gross Monthly Income	$_____
Net Monthly Income	$_____
Cash taken**	$_____
Deposit checking	$_____
Deposit savings	$_____
Other_____	$_____

** Cash breakdown for the month

Money Magnet (10%) of net	$_____
Mad Money	$_____
Food	$_____
Gas	$_____
Other_____	$_____

Pay Off Your Debt Worksheet –
Refer to Chapter Nine

Here is your form to track your payments for your debts, credit cards, student loans, car loans, personal debts, and any other amounts that you owe to someone else (everything but the mortgage). List your debts from smallest to largest, your minimum monthly payment, and the total amount you owe on each one.

Each month you will pay the minimum amount due on every bill, except for the one at the top. Your top bill (the smallest one) will be the big target that you will pay as much as you can towards each month—as much as you can afford. So, that means you pay the minimum due plus whatever amount you have left over from your budget after the essentials. And you pay this amount each month until it is paid off. Next, you take the amount you paid on the first bill and add that to your minimum payment for the next debt in line.

Each time you pay off a bill in full, you cross it off your list and add that payment to the next one until you have paid off everything. Oh yeah, and don't charge anything new while you are in this process. Get rid of your credit cards and use cash, checks, or debit card for your expenses each month. Follow your budget. Trust me, once you start this process and can cross off some of these line items, you will be hooked! It feels really good to pay off debt. When you are completely debt free, you will feel lighter and a lot more empowered with your money.

Debts Min. Mo. Payment Add-on Payment Total Amt. Due

*List smallest to largest

	Min. Mo. Payment	Add-on Payment	Total Amt. Due
_____	\$_____	\$_____	\$_____
_____	\$_____	\$_____	\$_____
_____	\$_____	\$_____	\$_____
_____	\$_____	\$_____	\$_____
_____	\$_____	\$_____	\$_____
_____	\$_____	\$_____	\$_____
_____	\$_____	\$_____	\$_____
_____	\$_____	\$_____	\$_____
_____	\$_____	\$_____	\$_____
_____	\$_____	\$_____	\$_____
_____	\$_____	\$_____	\$_____
_____	\$_____	\$_____	\$_____
_____	\$_____	\$_____	\$_____
_____	\$_____	\$_____	\$_____
_____	\$_____	\$_____	\$_____
_____	\$_____	\$_____	\$_____
_____	\$_____	\$_____	\$_____
_____	\$_____	\$_____	\$_____
_____	\$_____	\$_____	\$_____
_____	\$_____	\$_____	\$_____
_____	\$_____	\$_____	\$_____
_____	\$_____	\$_____	\$_____
_____	\$_____	\$_____	\$_____

Debts   Min. Mo. Payment Add-on Payment Total Amt. Due
*List smallest to largest

	$	$	$
	$	$	$
	$	$	$
	$	$	$
	$	$	$
	$	$	$
	$	$	$
	$	$	$
	$	$	$
	$	$	$
	$	$	$
	$	$	$
	$	$	$
	$	$	$
	$	$	$
	$	$	$
	$	$	$
	$	$	$
	$	$	$
	$	$	$
	$	$	$
	$	$	$
	$	$	$
	$	$	$
	$	$	$
	$	$	$
	$	$	$
	$	$	$
	$	$	$

Retirement Formula Sheet –
Refer to Chapter Nine

To determine how much money you will need in your retirement accounts by the time you retire, there is a simple formula. First, decide how much annual income you want to have each year when you retire. Let's say you want $50,000 or $100,000 income annually. We are not taking into consideration any Social Security income in this scenario. If Social Security is still around when you retire, then you will have a larger principal amount of money in your retirement accounts than you might need by then. At that point, you can decide if you want to take out less each year from your retirement accounts, or leave it in there to take care of your later needs, or leave it to your family or beneficiaries after your death.

Okay, so you want to have $100,000 per year income and you should calculate an average of 8% return per year on your investments in your retirement accounts. You might get more or less per year, but this is an average. Divide your desired annual income by .08 and you will get your number.

$$\$50,000 \div .08 = \$625,000$$
or
$$\$100,000 \div .08 = \$1,200,000$$

And so on—you simply divide your desired annual income by .08, reflecting an 8% return on your money. If you think you will get more than 8%, than divide your desired annual income by that percentage. In the example below we show what a 12% return would look like.

$$\$50,000 \div .12 = \$416,666$$
or
$$\$100,000 \div .12 = \$833,333$$

As you can see, the higher your percentage return on your investments, the less money you need in your accounts to work with. You should make this decision yourself, and I would suggest you talk to your financial advisor about the realistic returns to expect. I personally am basing my return on the lower end of 8%.

Your Get Well Plan –
Refer to Chapter Fifteen

MAKE A LIST HERE OF WHAT YOU WANT IN your life. Include tangible and non-tangible things. Include the goals, dreams, experiences, and assets you want in your life.

LIST OF ITEMS   EST. VALUE

Financial List:

_____	$_____
_____	$_____
_____	$_____
_____	$_____
_____	$_____
_____	$_____
_____	$_____
_____	$_____
_____	$_____
_____	$_____

Sub-Total $_____

Emotional/Mental List:

_____ $_____
_____ $_____
_____ $_____
_____ $_____
_____ $_____
_____ $_____
_____ $_____
_____ $_____
_____ $_____
_____ $_____

              Sub-Total $_____

Physical List:

_____ $_____
_____ $_____
_____ $_____
_____ $_____
_____ $_____
_____ $_____
_____ $_____
_____ $_____
_____ $_____
_____ $_____

              Sub-Total $_____

Experiences List:

_____ $_____
_____ $_____
_____ $_____
_____ $_____
_____ $_____
_____ $_____
_____ $_____
_____ $_____
_____ $_____
_____ $_____

Sub-Total $_____

Spiritual List:

_____ $_____
_____ $_____
_____ $_____
_____ $_____
_____ $_____
_____ $_____
_____ $_____
_____ $_____
_____ $_____
_____ $_____

Sub-Total $_____

Giving List:

_____ $_____
_____ $_____
_____ $_____
_____ $_____
_____ $_____
_____ $_____
_____ $_____
_____ $_____
_____ $_____
_____ $_____

Sub-Total $_____

Other:

_____ $_____
_____ $_____
_____ $_____
_____ $_____
_____ $_____
_____ $_____
_____ $_____
_____ $_____
_____ $_____
_____ $_____

Sub-Total $_____

TOTAL: $_____

Hire Michele to Speak at Your Event!

Michele Ashby's story of going from middle class to millionaire is both inspiring and engaging. Michele *comes out of the closet, shares her secrets* and encourages you to start talking about money. She discloses to her audiences what most millionaires won't— that gaining wealth is both an internal and external process.

Michele shares tips and tricks she has learned on her own personal journey, so that you can begin to live free of debt and worry. You will come away with new ideas to make your money behave differently and to acquire a life of financial freedom. You will be inspired to take control of your money matters so that you too may live the life you dream of, have the things you want, and even travel to wherever your heart desires.

To book Michele for your next event, please contact her directly at michele@ashbyinvestmentsllc.com

www.ingramcontent.com/pod-product-compliance
Lightning Source LLC
Chambersburg PA
CBHW030917180526
45163CB00002B/370